Praise for *Laser Quit Smoking Massage*

"Cole Nowicki's *Laser Quit Smoking Massage* examines the externalized oddities of late-stage capitalism to illuminate the tiered pathos of our everyday, autopay existence. In short, morse code bursts of measured madness, Nowicki transmits life from Canada's rural west with acerbic, unflinching prose, upturning every aspect of labor and its impact on family, identity and humanity's willingness to wait in line for the stench of a celebrity flower. A stunner of a collection, punching in equal parts laughter and profundity, Nowicki heals (laser patent pending)."

JOSÉ VADI, author of *CHIPPED: Writing from a Skateboarder's Lens & Inter State: Essays from California.*

"The essays in *Laser Quit Smoking Massage* are driven by the same gleeful curiosity that compels children to hunt for bugs in the tall grass. But instead of crickets or pillbugs, Nowicki uncovers missing relatives, dodgy home-based businesses, inexplicable urination, celebrity mentors, and yes, lasers. By holding a magnifying glass to these simple finds, they become complex, captivating, strange, and yet entirely relatable, all examined with empathy, warmth, and buoyant humour."

CHRISTOPHER EVANS, author of *Nothing Could Be Further from the Truth*

"Small town, big feelings. Cole Nowicki's essays are an album of memories: moments in time, crisp at the edges, bright with love, and some, bent in the middle by the type of grief one can only hope will smooth out with the unrelenting passage of time. Warm, sardonic, gentle, and human. (Lac La) Biche, you better buy this book!"

ALICIA TOBIN, comedian and author of *So You're A Little Sad, So What?*

"Urban poodle art, corpse flowers, and Craigslist's enduring humanity. These are the things that keep Cole Nowicki up at night. With warmth and wisdom to spare, Nowicki takes readers through a mix of imaginative and deeply entertaining topics. This is not just an essay collection, it's a guidebook of curiosities and family histories usually reserved for locals. *Laser Quit Smoking Massage* is a lozenge of literary absurdity that might just as soon sell you a watch as blow your mind."

CARLEIGH BAKER, award winning author of *Bad Endings*

"What a satisfying read *Laser Quit Smoking Massage* is. Cole Nowicki brings his sharp intelligence, sense of humor, and eye for unusual detail to a range of strange situations and in each case he comes away with something unexpected. The pieces are rich and complex, and like prose poems or flash fiction, they find their power in surprising turns and resonant imagery. "I wanted to bring beauty to this world," Nowicki writes. And in this pithy and poignant collection, he has."

JEN CURRIN, author of *Trinity Street* and *Hider/Seeker*

LASER

QUIT

SMOKING

MASSAGE

Laser Quit Smoking Massage

COLE

NOWICKI

Library and Archives Canada Cataloguing in Publication
Title: Laser quit smoking massage / Cole Nowicki.
Names: Nowicki, Cole, author.
Identifiers: Canadiana (print) 20230451233 | Canadiana (ebook) 20230451357 | ISBN 9781774390900
   (softcover) | ISBN 9781774390917 (EPUB)
Subjects: LCGFT: Essays.
Classification: LCC PS8627.O95 L37 2024 | DDC C814/.6—dc23

Editor for the Press: Thea Bowering
Cover design: Hiller Goodspeed
Interior Design: Meredith Thompson
Author Photo: Grady Mitchell

NeWest Press wishes to acknowledge that the land on which we operate is Treaty 6 territory and a traditional meeting ground and home for many Indigenous Peoples, including Cree, Saulteaux, Niitsitapi (Blackfoot), Métis, Dene, and Nakota Sioux since time immemorial. ||

NeWest Press acknowledges the support of the Canada Council for the Arts, the Alberta Foundation for the Arts, and the Edmonton Arts Council for support of our publishing program. This project is funded in part by the Government of Canada.

201, 8540–109 Street
Edmonton, Alberta T6G 1E6
780.432.9427
www.newestpress.com

No bison were harmed in the making of this book.

Printed and bound in Canada.   1 2 3 4   27 26 25 24

For the people and places that shape me <3

CONTENTS

Towns & Cities

1   Pride and Plockwurst

5   Commiserating

11   The Pile

17   Misadventure, Probably Drowning

23   Ray Liotta

27   How to Forget

31   Time Travel Concerns

35   Rona Oasis

41   Laser Quit Smoking Massage

49   Uncle Fester

55   The Dark Lord of Vancouver Karaoke

61   The Big Dog in the Sky is Dirty

67   Magic

Online & Forever

75   Pink Field

81   In the Galaxy Light of the Miracle

87   Amazing Facts About Camels

93   A Brief History of People Finding Weird Shit in Their Ears

99   Trolling in the Name of Art

105   The Last Wholesome Corner of the Internet

109   Send Flowers

115   My Personal Medium, Brian Eno

121   Things You Can Now Shoot Lasers At

127   Who Pissed On My Balcony

131   Smooth Black Marble

139   Instances of Birds in Peril

Thank Yous

Notes

TOWNS & CITIES

PRIDE AND PLOCKWURST

SMALL TOWN PRIDE TENDS to be a desperate thing, like searching for shore crabs under beach rocks. Some towns have it and we admire the tiny crabs for their surprising complexity or cuteness, but some on the ground in those communities use it as a tool to keep themselves sane or to drum up tourists, pulling the crabs apart leg by leg, in hopes of finding any morsel of meat that can be fried up, shared on Instagram, or milked for a buck. A truck stop in Valleyview, AB (population 1,849) was voted the best public bathroom in Canada in 2013, and the highway signs 20km out from the county limit make sure to let you know.

Small town pride is also distinct from the big city variety. Bigger city centres don't tend to have as much of an issue when it comes to creating community pride. The population density means more opportunities to foster culture, to have major sports teams, and a higher likelihood of infamous musicians or murderers calling them home. Those are things people and their pride naturally rally around. They add to a city's identity, and identity is key when dealing in pride.

Vancouver is green. Calgary is sprawling and littered with cowpeople. Hamilton is ... Hamilton, for better or worse. And sometimes "worse" adds definition. Look at Ottawa, our perennially touted capital of boring. "Worse" is an identity. How can the teensy town of Boyle, AB, stir pride in its ranks when it really doesn't have much of an identity at all due to its sheer dearth of populace?

If you know anything about Boyle, it's likely because you're googling it right now. And that's a big, bristling "if." An "if" as big as the big, bristling mustache of Justice John Robert Boyle, the former Alberta Liberal Party leader and Minister of Education from whom the town gets its name—which is almost interesting. Unfortunately, no one cares about ol' J.R Boyle and that's when small towns start reaching to make their toilets best in show.

Greater Napanee, Ontario, is a self-described "historic town" of nearly 17,000. If Greater Napanee sounds familiar, that's because it's where Canadian pop music icon Avril Lavigne was raised. The city of Greater Napanee's website, as it should, used to promote Avril like she was at city hall handing out black eyeliner and studded bracelets to every tourist who passed through. The town has a local talent whose success it can capitalize on and be proud of. Put her on billboards, manhole covers, and the official city seal. She's why people know the name Greater Napanee and not Boyle.

I'm from a small town that has nothing akin to an Avril, either. Lac La Biche, Alberta, is a community that isn't notable for anything besides being the current home of my grandmother, which isn't notable but should be because she's a wonderful person. The last rallying point of town pride I caught wind of from Lac La Biche was when a Boston Pizza opened up shop in 2011. That was big. Old classmates on Facebook gleefully planned on making it the next after-work, game, and wedding hotspot.

I was proud of Lac La Biche, too. We'd made it and had the Jambalaya Fettuccini to prove it. I even felt an odd bit of pride when, a couple of months after it opened, a pickup truck backed through the restaurant's front doors in the middle of the night, and a few masked men stole its ATM—ain't no big city restaurant going to change my town.

Unfortunately, that small-town-pride model is one of blanket homogenization. As in, "Let's bring in all the ubiquitous box stores and chain restaurants because that's what the people in other towns with more people like." Other more creative towns, towns that are generally lacking the promising oil sands capital of Lac La Biche, have to go out of their way to separate themselves from their neighbours in an effort to drum up town pride and tourists—and that's where wild, wanton ideas of townsfolk become a strange, surprising reality.

Vegreville, Alberta, is home to the world's second-largest Pysanka, a 2.5-tonne Ukrainian Easter egg. (The largest was built into the Pysanka Museum in Kolomyia, Ukraine, in 2000, nearly thirty years after Vegreville's was erected.) Duncan, BC, boasts a really big hockey stick that you might be interested in looking at for a few minutes. Sometimes the gimmicks aren't things but the names of towns themselves. There are small communities in Alberta named Excelsior, Vulcan and Balzac. Excelsior just sounds cool, Vulcan has had a Star Trek makeover and hosts an annual "Spock Days" festival that attracts Trekkies from all over the world, and Balzac is named after noted French novelist Honoré de Balzac. But mostly, the name just sounds like "ballsack." It's those odd, sometimes grandiose twists that make these small towns compelling.

But for me, the highest point any town has reached in the hunt for pride and identity comes from Mundare, Alberta. Mundare is the home of Stawnichy's Meat Processing. If you don't eat meat, I'm sorry you're missing out on those compacted tubes of ground-up animal nirvana. But it's not their sausages that I find so intriguing, it's how the town chose to celebrate them. In 2001, after forty years of turning animals into various delectable edible shapes, Stawnichy's and Mundare erected a commemorative 42 ft tall fibreglass kielbasa statue. A statue that looks less like a sausage and more like King Kong left the world's largest freestanding turd in the middle of an open field and just walked off.

It's that brand of blithe idealism that so willfully ignores aesthetic taste or good judgment that resonates with the small-town roots in me. I'm not from Mundare, but in a sense, I feel like I am. That four-storey sausage is the town punching up and back at the city—its pickup truck through the front doors of the Boston Pizza. Edmonton can build a gargantuan mall and tourists will flock to Orange Julius and get day-drunk in the wave pool, but Mundare has taken a symbolic shit on its community as if to let the world know that they're happy with the little mess they've made for themselves and they want you to come see it. They even built it an observation deck. And while most of us would try our best to hold back our twelve-year-old selves from calling it the "poop deck," I'm sure most Mundare residents stand on it, in the shadow of their titanic sausage, looking out over the parking lot of the neighbouring Esso station, with pride.

COMMISERATING

"Oh, dude. So sorry. It sucks that this is happening to you right now," I tell the Skittle as I hold it between my fingers: me, a giant with Jack's future in the pad of my thumb. I'm apologizing because the piece of candy is on trial and it had no idea. It wasn't informed that it had a say in its future and is now desperate. The Skittle tries to reason, to plead its case to me, a child sprawled out on the off-white carpeted floor of his childhood bedroom. It tells me about its friends—*sure, they're sour, but I love them!* and how they have soccer practice that night and it's an important one because they're going to a tournament in Vegreville that weekend and they really need to work on their defence.

Deliberating, I roll the Skittle between my fingers like a booger. Its sugary colouring stains the tips.

"So, you're telling me your friendships and extra-curricular sporting activities are your only worth?"

Panicked, it shakes its head—which is its whole being—and spews out its hopes and dreams. How it wants to write books, travel the world with its skateboard, and fall in love. These are all reasonable, desirable things. And I am empathetic; I really am. I know what it's like to dream. To want something that seems so far away. But reality is blunt and unflinching in its honesty. The cracked and gravelly streets of Lac La Biche, Alberta, are shit to skateboard on and I don't have a way out, either. All I have are the stories I scribble into my little Five Star notepad. Love, however, is out of the question for me. "I'm ten, much too young for that," I tell the Skittle. It nods because it doesn't know what else to do.

"Okay, glad we're on the same page." Those words are a gavel as I toss the candy into the air, catching it in my mouth, cracking its sweet shell with my teeth, and sucking on the innards like a juvenile vampire. I continued being judge, jury, and masticator as my three-disc stereo switched CDs to Blink-182's *Enema of the State*. My preteen self was already immune to their songs' many, many curses and references to masturbation. There was a point when they were novel, though. My friends and I in the playground reciting with glee the lyrics to "Family Reunion"— the band's rendition of comedian George Carlin's "Seven Dirty Words" bit. But that time had passed. I'd matured and begun to enjoy the subtleties of their canon. The dark honesty of "Adam's Song" and the intergalactic longing of "A New Hope."

Even their big hits had nuggets to unpack. It took hundreds of listens before I finally registered that in the lyrics of "All the Small Things," they use the word "commiserating."

Commiserating. *Commiserating?* What did that word mean? I didn't know Blink to have a vocabulary that expanded much beyond "nah, nah, nah, nah, nah." I felt the excitement of having discovered something: a treasure waiting to be had. Each letter of the word was a link in a priceless gold chain, but I needed its definition to truly measure its worth. Out in the living room my mother sat on the couch reading. Whether through genetics or verbal osmosis, her love of words had been passed on to me. The pleasure she'd get from deploying a juicy word into conversation was obvious.

"Those Beavis and Butthead are filth—they're truly *anathema* to me." She'd say sternly, satisfied.

If anyone knew what *commiserating* meant, it'd be her. This could also be a moment to legitimize my favourite band, whom she often proclaimed was vulgar, stupid, and whose compact discs she would routinely threaten to throw in the garbage because she believed they were eating away at the tender meat of my mortal soul. If they used words like "commiserating," they must have some deeper appreciation for language, as we did.

I poke her shoulder and the question blurts out between the slats of my stupid, toothy grin. I can't contain it. I am a ten-year-old, absolutely fired up for words and knowledge. She slowly closes her book, a lone finger saving the page, before turning to look me in the eyes.

"That is not a word."

She turns back and I stammer out a defence. I know what I heard. Yeah, their songs are silly, but that doesn't mean they still can't have depth! My endorsements are not enough. She is unmoved and the book open again in her lap. Argument over.

Invalidating truth isn't difficult. All one has to do is choose not to believe. A person can even know something's true; they just have to keep that truth inside and stow it away someplace sealed with pride, ignorance, shame, or whatever it may be. The facts may even be directly in front of them—burned onto a five-time- platinum-selling

CD their child has had on repeat for nearly two years. The reasons behind those denials are trickier.

Confusion mixes with the tepid rush of validation and embarrassment once I find "commiserating" in Webster's Dictionary. Why would she lie? If she didn't know, couldn't she just say so? I commiserate with myself, eat more Skittles, and ask them these questions before delivering their tasty, but ultimately final, verdict. I have sympathy for the candies and the little lives I'd given to and taken from them. I commiserate with the rest of the Skittles in the bag each time I down one.

"Sorry, everyone. I know this is a tough time—for all of us."

I commiserate with an entire handful, a colourful stream pouring into my mouth as I lie on the floor. But the Skittles ignore my compassion and revolt, slipping past my tongue, which had up until then served as shepherd and executioner positioning the candies into rows beneath guillotine molars. The candies fall directly down my throat. I know I am choking before I attempt a breath. The realization happens in slow motion, like a sugary car crash, Skittles clicking off one another deep within my airway like debris from colliding SUVs.

As I gasp, my three-disc stereo switches to Linkin Park and it becomes apparent that I'm going to die. This is the soundtrack of the damned in the early aughts. I roll around on the carpet, doing a high-stakes interpretation of the worm. It doesn't help. I try to wheeze one simple, pitiful breath, and the Skittles suck together tighter, sealing off my lungs.

Linkin Park's "Crawling" oozes through the stereo speakers as I crawl to the bed, which, if I weren't choking, I'd probably find poetic. The bee-booping of the synth leads to a crush of nü-metal guitar as I struggle to get up. First, to my knees, then my feet. Suddenly, I'm off of the ground. Lifted by the clasped hands of my mom performing the Heimlich. One, two, three squeezes and the Skittle obstruction crumbles; the candies tumble out of me, landing in a sticky pile on the carpet. It burns. My mom holds me, her eyes wide as she asks if I'm okay.

It's the same look as when I fell down the basement stairs the winter before. I'd been running back down to the TV, the commercial break during my Saturday morning cartoons almost over. Halfway down, I tripped and cleared the remaining stairs to the linoleum below. The oversized mug of chocolate milk I'd rushed up the stairs to get spread from my body like blood. My mom had been in the garage but said she felt something. A pang. Some sort of motherly alert that told her to go inside, where she found her son whimpering in a pool of chocolate. She brought me to the bathroom, washed my face, asked me if I was okay, promised me I would be alright.

We sit on the bed. She had already collected all of the offending Skittles, tossed them into the garbage, and used a rag to scrub at the bright stains left on the carpet. The stereo switches CDs to Blink-182's *Dude Ranch*. She does not tell me to change it or remind me of their vulgarity and stupidity. We just listen as she strokes my hair. She tells me she needs me to be more careful, not with anger but concern. She whispers that she's sorry this happened, feeling pain for something she did not do. "Sorry, my sweet," she says. "I'm so sorry."

THE PILE

THERE IS A LUMP of twenty-dollar bills in my bedside table drawer. It's not a neat stack. Hastily assembled, its haphazard state may seem to indicate a lack of care or direction; but I withdrew this money for a purpose: booze.

In an effort to stop using my debit card at the bar—a financially dangerous arrangement that allows one to pay for pints without seeing the damage done to one's bank account—I created the money pile. I pay for my nights out only with The Pile. The Pile is my nightlife lifeline. I can enjoy myself only if The Pile is full, healthy, towering. I do not take the entire pile with me when I go out. Just bits. Scoops. Handfuls. This, in theory, teaches me moderation. Pace yourself with The Pile. Do not spread The Pile thin. You always want to be able to stand high atop The Pile, looking out at all of the Good Times ahead.

Sometimes it's hard to recognize the Good Times, even when you're smack in the middle of them—especially once you've gone through a dollop or two of The Pile. The horizon becomes hazy, fog rolls in, and you forget what you're supposed to be seeing, so you dig into The Pile again.

* * *

I am running towards The Pile—quick, even paces from Labone's Kitchen and Bar back to my apartment. My friends at the bar aren't beholden to any wild mounds of loose bills, so they order round after round of anything they want—bloated Albertan oilfield paycheques easily covering the cost of the alcoholic overhead required to survive in that world. Weeks on weeks of living in camps in the middle of the wild, working gruelling hours, with soured testosterone permeating nearly every human interaction, leaves Jägerbombs and cocaine purchased from some guy whose cousin in The City who has the hook up on that supposed *good shit*, as the only release.

When I told my friends that I'd be back, that I had to go consult The Pile, a mass of currency that decides the fate of my nights, they said:

"I got you, buddy!"

"Lemme get you sumthin'!"

"Are u fuck'n stoopid, it's mine-us twenny-sis outsigh."

—their swollen wallets were boils that needed to be lanced by charity.

"C'mon, pleeeeeeeaze. Lemme get this one fer u, man."

"Dudeeeeeeeeeeeeeee, yu gotta, u gotta."

I respectfully declined. It's a thing of principle. I would get *myself* wasted, thank you very much. Now I am running, thanks to my principles and because my conception of proper winter attire is not in line with what's required in a bitter Albertan February at 12 AM. Toque. Wool sweater. Jeans. Skate shoes. I was born in Lac La Biche and lived there for most of my childhood, but I dress like I've been ejected early from an airplane destined for Seattle.

The painfully wool collar on my excruciatingly wool sweater works as a Brillo pad on my neck as I huff to the apartment. I can feel goose pimples being scrubbed away raw. I tell myself I'm making good time, but my understanding of time itself is skewed, the beer that The Pile afforded me shoving back the clock's second hand as the shots of bourbon my cursedly wealthy friends bought me put the minute hand in a full nelson.

For how long I think I've been pushing my way through the frigid night, it's surprising I haven't noticed the group behind me, sooner. And when I do see them, I am surprised and, for whatever reason, embarrassed that these folks have been watching my progressively deteriorating speed-hobble. I slow to a walk. Casual. Cold. Freezing cold. With each extension, my knees lock frozen, like a cup of water tossed into arctic air. I occasionally look back at the group, who don't seem to mind my gait, considering they are getting closer.

When I finally reach the walkway of my apartment building, three young men corral me, their respective girlfriends standing off to the side, dutifully watching an assault transpire. The young man in front of me asks for my money. I politely let him know that I do not have any, as I've spent it all at the bar, which is why they saw me sprinting through the snow like a Whitetail fawn stumbling on newborn legs right through their sights. But they don't seem to understand. He asks again, this time with a shove. His friend to my right punctuates the request with a "Yah, bitch."

I try to explain to them the concept of The Pile. How the budgeting system I've created for myself is designed for me to return home without any cash on hand. They do not care for what, I believe, is a rather ingenious method. They keep asking. Demanding.

"I do not have any money on my person," I tell them each time. "*I do not have any money on my person.*"

They get louder and louder until the young man in front of me snaps, sucker-punches me in the jaw, tells me to "shut the fuck up," and walks off with his guys, their girlfriends shuffling along the icy sidewalk in their wake—and that's it. It's over. No follow-up punches or monetary requests. I watch them leave, confused. Angry. Cold. Itchy from the wool. I feel like I could've done better. Like I could've, should've fought back. Three dudes? I've seen MMA; I had that. The farther they walk down the sidewalk, the more my confidence grows until I am warm—steamy with rage. Molten revenge roiling. Then they stop. Turn. Take a right down a walkway to the second entrance of my apartment building. My assailants, my neighbours.

* * *

My apartment is much too small. It cannot contain the heaving, writhing animal I've become. A creature punched into being. I careen through the living room, slide across the walls, grip the kitchen counter with rage:

"Fuckin' fuckers!"

"They shunta dunn that!"

"I know where yew live, dummies!"

I take out my flip phone and try to find my brother's number. He is also my roommate, but I know he isn't home because his room is the first one I burst into once back in the apartment. A primal scream escapes me as I see his unmade bed. The names in my contact list bleed together through digital osmosis. Unreadable. I flip my phone closed violently, imagining every letter from every word from every text I've ever sent, tumbling to the bottom of their respective threads in a heap. I slap myself in the face. I don't need help. I will do it myself. As I leave the apartment, I remind myself again of the MMA I've watched, vengeance imminent.

* * *

Gentle. Gentle. Gentle. Gently I place my ear to each door in my building, like a nosy, tip-toeing toddler. Listening for the voices of the men who jumped me. What happens when I do hear the familiar baritone of "Yah, bitch"? I've already got that figured out:

Step 1. Knock on door.

Step 2. When they answer, say, "Sorry to bother you at this hour, sir, but I'd like to have a word with you and your friends re: the event that took place earlier this evening."

Step 3. Kick their goddamn fucking asses.

I recite Step 2. to myself as I navigate the first, second and third floors. My ear suction-cupped to each apartment door. Only once do I think I hear the "Yah, bitch" guy, which turns out just to be a Letterman monologue that makes me laugh to the hallway, empty except for me. By the time I've eavesdropped on every suite in the building, the molten rage inside me has begun to cool, leaving behind a mess of hard, heavy rocks. Too much to carry. At the top of the stairwell, I slide to the floor and close my eyes.

* * *

There are no dreams, just a heavy curtain of black. I can hear the building move and creak, speaking to itself. Its pipes whirring with some benign banter. I listen to this conversation until it is no longer lulling and just dull. I make my way back to my apartment. Inside, my brother is laughing with a friend. He asks me where I've been, what I've been doing, why I looked so fucked. I try to tell him, but all that comes out are charred stones in an angry, unintelligible jumble. I step to him, words falling from my mouth, failing to form. So, I punch him. Hard. Right in the nose. Then stagger to my room, close the door and drop into bed. The Pile sits comfortably in the bedside table. Full. Healthy. Listening to the ragged sound of my breath until it becomes even, consistent, moderated.

MISADVENTURE, PROBABLY DROWNING

ZIGMUND NOWICKI DISAPPEARED IN 1961. I didn't know Zigmund Nowicki existed until 2018. He was a great-uncle whose name I'd never heard until a chance utterance around the dinner table while I was back in Alberta for my younger sibling's high school graduation.

Oh, Ziggy? Grandpa had another brother. Where is he? No one knows for sure. He went missing.

And that was that. A mystery stated as fact that required no further inquiry. I'd pick up more details as the months went on, prodding my parents. The prevailing story was that Ziggy worked up in Uranium City, Saskatchewan, as a bus driver in the late '50s and early '60s, shuttling workers to and from the uranium mine each day. Then, one weekend, a few years before my father was born, Ziggy went into the woods and never returned. He was twenty-five years old.

When my parents were still together, my mother had asked her mother-in-law, my grandmother, about Ziggy. She got the same truncated story along with the directive to never bring it up around my grandfather. She never did. And from my understanding, no one else did either, which makes sense. That something or someone as mysterious and engaging as Ziggy would go unmentioned in our family is not surprising. The Nowicki brand of stoicism is frustratingly strong. If you tell us that your appendix burst, but you'd prefer we don't tell anyone, we won't enjoy watching you go septic, but we also won't call an ambulance out of respect.

And for decades, no one dug at this uncertainty. My grandparents had three more boys after my father. Eight grandchildren. They worked until their sixties: Grandpa, a heavy-duty mechanic who sacrificed his knees to his profession; Grandma, a schoolteacher in the age of yardstick discipline. (Grown men she taught thirty years previous still take their hats off and look to the ground in deference as she passes.)

All of this life happened without mention of Ziggy's own.

✳ ✳ ✳

I wasn't the only one poking at the past. After some online sleuthing, my sister discovered *Uranium City: The Last Boom Town,* in the University of Alberta's online library. Written by Bernard Garnet McIntyre and published in 1993, the book details the history of Uranium City from its boom to its inevitable bust and transition into a contemporary ghost town.

"The Search for Ziggy Nowicki" is Chapter 36 in McIntyre's book. There are four pages dedicated to my great uncle's disappearance. In those two spreads, we learn that he was affable, beloved in the community, and that when he went missing, over 100 people scoured the woods looking for him. At 28 years old, my grandfather travelled north and searched for his younger brother for weeks but could not find him, a brutal northern Saskatchewan winter eventually turning him back.

The book tells how Ziggy brought his 8mm film camera into the woods and how a duo of prospectors, Sidney Hawker and Jim Wan, would eventually find it six years after Ziggy's disappearance. The camera was placed neatly beside a backpack that held a couple of rusted cans of beans, a .22 calibre rifle, and a hunting knife stained with blood and stuck with feathers. But that was all they found. No remains. The RCMP tried to develop the film in the camera, but its exposure to a half-dozen winters had spoiled it. Any answers it held had expired.

One Easter, I went back to Lac La Biche and visited the family farm, the home of an uncle and aunt once my grandparents moved into assisted living. My sister's find had piqued the curiosity of some family members, and now other bits of Ziggy-related information began to surface over dinner. Conspiracy theories. Another uncle, who'd worked up in northern Saskatchewan decades previous, recalled a passing conversation with a man on his crew who grew up in Uranium City and was a child when Ziggy went missing.

The city had whispered about the incident for years, he told my uncle, hinting that Zigmund's end was of nefarious means—but the two were interrupted before the man could go into detail. Then there were the whispers within our family. I heard a rumour from my sister, who heard it from my father, who'd heard it over the years: that Ziggy faked his death and ran off.

Those theories were tantalizing and morbidly fun to think about, in the way conspiracies can be, but they were otherwise moot—ultimately, we knew what happened. At the end of

Ziggy's chapter in *The Last Boom Town*, McIntyre reports that a few months after the discovery of Ziggy's belongings, Sidney Hawker's brother, Ashton, "found a human skull lying in the swampy area between Fold and Coe lakes." Less than a mile from where my great uncle's things were found. The RCMP returned and searched the area, finding more bones and a wristwatch later identified as Ziggy's. With that evidence, the coroner declared him "legally dead ... by misadventure, probably drowning."

✳ ✳ ✳

On the farm, in an old grain shed that now stores mostly junk, mice, and mice pellets, we piled around a dusty metal trunk containing all of Ziggy's belongings gathered from Uranium City. In it were old newspapers, stamps, and his shaving kit—expected things. Then there was the empty engagement ring box and dozens of letters from a fiancé, Arlene, whom none of us had known about. The letters detailed her loneliness as Ziggy regularly "went away": in one instance, on a solo vacation to Mexico. Arlene detailed her depression as she struggled to finish painting the kitchen cupboards. How she wouldn't be surprised if his family didn't pick him, "Mr. Big Shot," up at the airport on his way back from vacation, "since he'd disappointed them all so much."

There were Polaroids of who we assumed to be Arlene with a small child. Ziggy's? No one knew. Among the letters were Ziggy's old pay stubs, receipts, and notices from his employer that he owed them money. It was crowded in the shed as we pored over the artifacts and marvelled at all of the unknown becoming known. I opened a leather folder and the room went quiet. It was a life insurance policy issued about a year before Ziggy's disappearance. We already had conspiratorial embers burning, but here was kindling and kerosene. *Had Ziggy actually faked his own death? And run away? To Mexico? For insurance money?*

Is this why our grandfather never talked about his missing brother? That pain less about his death and more about what was unsettled. Is that why his mother, my great-grandmother, worried until her last days that the bones in Ziggy's grave were not her son's? There was only something here if we chose to believe it. If we wanted to rip off a half-century-old scab and jump in. Would we tell Grandpa Ed, then immobile in assisted living, that we were looking into this? Into things he'd likely already looked into decades ago? Looking for answers that he had once spent weeks looking for in the woods of northern Saskatchewan, without success? Into a past that he'd rarely spoken of since?

Under the life insurance policy was a clear glass bottle. My aunt picked it up, rubbed the dust from it and peered at the gold-coloured powder inside as she tipped it from side to side, watching the granules slide. She wondered aloud what it was, the yellowcake uranium inches away from her face.

RAY LIOTTA

THERE ARE CERTAIN THINGS that can help improve your memory: meditation, eating right, a good night's rest, proper exercise of the body and the mind. But how many minutes of meditation does it take to remember to empty the compost? Does it require ten or fifteen bench press reps to dig the date of your mother's birthday out of the soft soil of your brain? Those methods require continued commitment, with varied, unsatisfying degrees of success.

* * *

"As far back as I could remember, I always wanted to be a gangster," says Henry Hill in the opening monologue of the 1990 mobster movie classic *Goodfellas*. From first watch at fourteen years old, the Scorsese masterpiece has stuck with me. The highly stylized ultra-violence and scorching profanity-laced dialogue was like nothing I had witnessed before. Henry's acute memory was at odds with the recall of my teenage self at the time. If someone shared a new name, date, lesson or anything of any level of importance with me, expecting it to find purchase in my prefrontal cortex, the information would smack against a combination of general teenage malaise and weed smoke, before falling like a robin crashing into a picture window and landing still in the shrubs below.

During that time, on a summer afternoon when even the lawn was too hot to touch, I lay on the couch in my parents' basement thinking about *Goodfellas*: The squelching sounds made by Joe Pesci's blade driving into the body of Billy Batts, "made man" of the Gambino crime family; the way the youth slowly drained from Henry as the movie progressed, paranoia causing his eyes to bulge and his once handsome features to warp and sag as his crimes tally up and the FBI closes in, until he finds himself in witness protection, grumpy and discontent at his new everyday life that's revealed in the film's waning seconds. These memories were unusually vivid and instant. I could almost see Henry with his thin lips pursed in front of me. What I couldn't remember was the name of the actor who played him.

Flopping back and forth on the couch, I tried to wrestle loose this bit of pop-culture trivia without the help of Google. The effort hurt my brain. I could feel the piece of grey matter where the name was supposed to be, dull and cold, like a dead bulb in a string of Christmas lights. My inability to remember was concerning to my prematurely fried self.

I pushed on my head for the rest of that day, hoping to squeeze out the answer. Nothing came. That night it was too humid to sleep and I wandered the house. In the bathroom, as I sat on the toilet in a grim silence, it finally appeared to me in bold, bright letters: *Ray Liotta. Ray Liotta.* I said it again and again. I chanted it as I washed my hands, chanted it while in bed, and promised myself I would never forget Ray Liotta's, or any other name, again.

* * *

Funerals are a celebration of memory. What was once a person is now just shared experience, which puts a high premium on one's ability to remember. A few months later, at the funeral of a distant great-aunt, people shared their stories into a microphone on a stage. I didn't know her well, so I only listened, the mourner's memories becoming mine. Afterwards, as we all approached the alive, distant great-uncle to offer condolences, I realized that even after an hour of listening to stories about the dead, distant great-aunt romping through fields as a child and being a wonderful, caring mother, friend, and colleague—I couldn't remember her name. The line to the distant great-uncle grew shorter and I knew I would have to say something, anything about her to him, and that referring to her by anything besides her name wasn't going cut it.

That's when the repetition began, the words throbbing close behind my skull. The line continued to shrink, and in between groups of steadily shuffling family members with damp, puffy eyes, I started to chant out loud, under my breath: *Ray Liotta, Ray Liotta, Ray Liotta.* By the time I reached the distant great-uncle, I found it—*my condolences; Marie was a wonderful person.* Ray's name was a tool I'd used to break into my own mind. Each iterance a new bend in the paperclip that wormed its way through the lock until it clicked.

Since then, Ray Liotta has been helping me resurface memories for nearly a decade. He's helped me out in exams, when I run into acquaintances and the name of their new experimental glitter-pop noise band has escaped me, and at parties when no one can remember who gets murdered first in *Scream 2*. He's been helping me remember with the immediacy and consistency that a healthy diet and fifteen minutes of an empty mind a day just cannot.

It almost feels like I'm cheating, as if I know the correct combination of buttons to press on the PlayStation controller—*R2, Square, Up, Down, Right, X*—then boom, *typhoid*. Typhoid was the disease Mary Mallon carried, and now I have my green slice of pie while everyone else playing Trivial Pursuit slaps their thighs in frustration at my continued success.

* * *

There are some questions, however, that Ray Liotta doesn't have the answer to, like: *how could you do that? Why didn't you call? Did you even consider how I'd feel?* And *why can't you say that you love me?* I still summon Ray for help on these, chanting as quietly as I can to myself, using up time that I don't have. But the Ray Liotta that answers isn't the spry, young Henry Hill from the beginning of *Goodfellas*; it's the weary, worn one in witness protection at the end. His bathrobe wrapped around himself as he stands on the stoop of his anonymous government-provided home, regretting the decisions he's made. And he never responds to me because Henry doesn't answer to that name anymore.

HOW TO FORGET

1. Find the location in your home that receives the most sunlight. Where the sun stretches across the floor, lie face down in its warmth. Let it weigh on you. Play the *M*A*S*H* theme song on repeat while lying there for approximately one hour or until the sunlight has moved.

2. While still on the floor, logroll into the kitchen. If the room in your home that receives the most sunlight is your kitchen, roll out of the kitchen and then back into it. Once finished, stand up and make something to eat. Do not eat the food. Instead, leave it on the counter for someone to find.

3. Go through the contact list on your phone. Whatever the first letter of the name of what or who you're trying to forget is, delete that entire letter section. Do the same with your iTunes library, Instagram, Twitter followers, and Facebook friends.

4. Call someone who is still in your contact list who is not the thing, or related to the thing, that you're trying to forget. Ask them how their day was. Ask

them what their weekend plans are. Ask them about their faith or lack thereof. Ask them if they're in love or ever have been. If they ask you those questions in return, tell them you are not comfortable with that line of questioning at the moment. Unless you are, then answer.

5. Take out the compost. Before you dump it into the bin outside, take a moment to look at the contents of the outside bin. Notice the banana peel in its state of decomposition. Consider how, even though its "fruit," its perceived purpose, has been eaten and therefore "served," it is still in use. Watch the worms and maggots writhe through the holes they've chewed in the peel. No matter how grisly, that is not the image of spent purpose. Repeat this to yourself.

6. Sit upside down on the sofa. Let the blood flow into and then pool in your head. Allow yourself to become lightheaded. Listen to the dull throb at your temples grow louder until you can no longer hear the vehicle and pedestrian traffic outside. Sit right side up.

7. With your arms, make small circles that slowly get larger and larger until you cannot go into any room in your house without knocking something over. Consider this a physical representation of the mental and emotional anguish that you are currently in.

8. Collect various reflective surfaces (mirrors, cutlery, tablet screens, etc.) and place them around you in a circle. Look into each reflective surface, one at a time. Notice how each offers a different perspective

of what you consider a constant: yourself. Reflect on this.

9. Search online for the website of the swanky condominiums being built across the street from your favourite coffee shop. Take a virtual tour of one of their two-bedroom condos. Imagine a life in which you live in this suite. You have a family. Your small child burbles in a high chair as you feed them. Ask yourself: what are you feeding your future child for dinner?

10. When no one comes home to ask what the food on the counter is doing there, explain softly to the room that it was for them.

TIME TRAVEL CONCERNS

MY GRANDPARENTS ARE TRAVELLING back in time. They're expected to land in 1945. The quaint, weathered home they'll arrive at as septuagenarians is the same house my Grandpa Barry spent his childhood in. There are seventy-some-odd years between then and now. On what seems like a whim, they have decided to pick up and move from the outskirts of Lac La Biche back to a smaller speck on the map: Sedgewick, Alberta. This house, at the mouth of a quiet cul-de-sac and dressed in peeling pale-blue siding, is the rocket sled from *Timecop*, Calvin's cardboard box—a bonafide time machine. Once they arrive, they'll muck up the timeline. My timeline.

***

For as long as I can remember, my grandparents have lived on a farm in a beautiful two-storey home that they built themselves. Multiple bedrooms, baths, and a shining solid wood staircase that winds its way up to the top floor. There's a solarium attached to the kitchen that feels almost alien, especially in the frigid Albertan winters—as a kid, I envisioned the shelves of blooming plant life inside it held captive species from far-off planets; the glass room was a laboratory, and my Grandmother a government official conducting top-secret experiments, watering can in hand.

Surrounding the house are acres of fields full of cows, hay bales and berry bushes that always required my immediate attention as springs moved into summers: stained fingers, raspberry red, a sign of a job well done.

My parents met on the patch of land where the farmhouse would later stand. Their respective families were neighbours just a few grassy hectares apart. My dad and his brothers were enlisted by their parents to help build my mother's home because that's what neighbours do. The walls and roof and hardwood floor and winding staircase—my parents helped piece them together. A number of years later, they worked together to build me. That house is the reason for my existence. Both sets of my grandparents are still friends to this day, remaining so even through their children's messy split and nearly fifty years of somehow just plain not getting sick of one another. But now? That's all going to be erased. What my grandparents have done by leaving the farm is walk backwards, retracing their steps through the years, across generations, and back into a former state of self. One that I don't belong to. I'll be gone. Marty McFly phased out of existence.

I should explain this worry of mine. My understanding is that time is a series of puddles in a gravel road. As you move along that road, glimpses of yourself, memories, are captured in the rainwater caught in the divots and tread marks. In some puddles, your face is clear, defined. You: mirrored in a moment that you can look back on. Other puddles are shallow or muddied, rocks and sticks obstructing the view—instances of little importance or of ones you'd rather forget.

But if you start to move backwards along that same road, like my grandparents are doing, you will step right in those puddles, and the memories they hold will sploosh out. Or they'll be shaken and erased like the fragile image in an Etch A Sketch. It's the same general premise Christopher Reeves employed, clad in Superman's blue tights and red cape while flying backwards around and around the earth, rolling linear time back up into a ball until he reached the moment in which he could save Lois Lane. Once he had, time was allowed to unravel again in a different direction.

I've done it in my own life, on a smaller scale. When I dropped out of university after only four months, and unceremoniously moved back home, it was like I'd never attempted higher education. Only a few murky memories remain: the saxophone-playing roommate I used to steal juice boxes from; and the time I skateboarded home from the grocery store loaded with bags and hit a pebble in front of the dorms. I did a baseball slide through my produce, warped the loaf of bread and popped a carton of OJ. When I got to my feet, I expected laughter from those smoking in the parking lot but got only whimpers of sympathy—these are the last remaining details of a period in my life that I've wiped clean from the docket via time travel. Those memories just embarrassing ghosts, flitting by.

My most successful instance of personal retcon came when our family cat died peacefully underneath my father's out-of-commission Oldsmobile, remaining forever frozen as if curled up on the couch. Four-year-old me would lie down on the gravel driveway every day to take in her long sleep. Returning to watch the grass grow around her as she sunk further into the earth. Her fur softer, lighter, until it was nothing at all. For months I went to the car to peek underneath, until it became habit: retracing and retreading the memory until it frayed, snapped, fell away, and I could no longer remember why I was in the dirt on my hands and knees.

* * *

Maybe I'm overreacting. It's not as though my grandparents are doing it on purpose. I doubt my grandfather wants to hit rewind and prune my branch of the family tree. They probably just want a little peace. A place for themselves without the demands of livestock and sundry human interaction. Who can blame them?

What I need to do now is live quickly. Be thankful. Make the most of what time I have left until they put their Ford Windstar in reverse and rip into the past. Bottoming out as they hit each pothole, memories splashing across the road and the van barrelling down it. Drops of me falling, then cleared away by windshield wipers. A streak of life, hard to make out, refracted by the sun.

RONA OASIS

I NEEDED TO RUN, SO I ran. Across the parking lot of Sherwood Park's RONA building centre to the display of sheds at one end (a nice selection of plastic and wooden structures, a variety of sizes, some with sliding doors, some hinged) and back to the van at the other end, where David was doing push-ups and Kohen stood smoking.

If you ask me why I needed to run, I couldn't tell you. It was just instinctual. Like breathing or love. However, the running was precipitated by a feeling that I can describe:

1. It started with a warmness of the chest. A hot orb that hung just behind the sternum.

2. Once the van was parked, the orb dislodged and began to move around the torso.

3. Outside of the van, as if provoked by exposure to the late-morning sun, the orb began to shake and fizz—pop-rocks dinging off the rib cage.

This overflow was followed by a rush of joy. Unadulterated. Overwhelming. Overriding my bodily autonomy and forcing me to jump out of the vehicle and run to the shed display and back.

At the van, post-dash, the joyful fizz settled. David had finished his push-ups and was now onto jumping jacks. While on the road, he had to improvise his daily exercise regime; the parking lots of liquor stores, venues where the band was playing, and now RONA were the only available spaces to work out. While waiting for Kohen to finish the last drags of his cigarette, the orb began to heat up and froth again. I had no choice. I started running in the direction of RONA's automated doors.

We were here to buy ratchet straps. The belongings we couldn't fit inside the van we'd wrapped in a tarp and tied to the roof, but the bundle had started to free itself as we drove through the unwavering grey of Edmonton's streets, the loose blue of the tarp slapping at passing vehicles. That blue, waving wildly from the top of the vehicle, was the only colour for blocks. The "grass" in the medians was a stiff medley of browns and yellows; the skeleton trees, stuck sporadically down a few choice city sidewalks, were patronizing at best.

In fairness, we'd arrived from Vancouver, whose vibrant, verdant streets seem almost, paradoxically, unnatural compared to those of other cities. The ubiquitous concrete hues of Edmonton's neighbourhoods all bleed into one another. Grey blood cells on grey blood cells on grey blood cells. Its asphalt arteries eventually bled us into the suburb of Sherwood Park, where we oozed into RONA's parking lot.

Despite the welcome chill of the air conditioning in the store, the orb continued to burn hot as it Plinko'd around my chest. I ran past pallets of fertilizer on special, in preparation for spring, my feet making surprisingly little sound on the polished concrete as I took wild, serpentine strides in the aisles. I ran past Matt as he stood in front of a towering wall of ratchet straps and then took turn, after turn, after turn.

In the electrical and lighting aisle, a string of chandeliers coated everything in a warm, artificial glow, which I preferred to the blandness of "Plumbing"—an aisle I sped up through. Here, I worked at a casual jog, reading the names on the tags of different fixtures before they slipped past my peripherals—*Catalina, Opus, Uberhaus, Lumirama*. Givers of Light deserved beautiful designations like these, I thought as I made my way into "Flooring and Ceramic Tile."

The various stains of hardwood on display were comforting. Strips of material just waiting to tie some recently retired couple's den together. "Heating, Cooling and Ventilation" was okay. The ducts, like clunky tin snake "moults," failed to capture my attention.

Back in the big, central aisle of the store, I alternated my pace, leapt over small displays of interior latex paints, used my footwork to outmaneuver an outdoor dining set. I did all of this without trouble from any employee or customer, making the RONA my personal parkour course, being driven by whatever inexplicable feeling I harboured. Was it a feeling of freedom from being out of the van, from being nearly out of the grey of the city, from being out on the road and away from the responsibilities of home? I tried to diagnose as I ran.

* * *

Once, in a bookstore in Montréal, I became similarly over-whelmed. Walking along its shelves, my fingers traced the spines of books by authors I knew and admired and ones by authors I didn't know but hoped I would. At that moment, my eyes began to well; and when the tears and *that* feeling arrived, I knew exactly why it had. It was all of the manifested potential captured in the books around me, this incredible mass of words detailing political theories, stories of love, struggle, creativity, recipes, dog breeds.

These books had started as ideas, then grew, found their way to the page, flourished and were now in my hands. The thought of that process, that potential, made me leak. As I entered RONA's garden centre—a sweltering, expansive greenhouse lined with rows and rows of potted plants, flowers and hanging baskets whose leaves hung right at head-tickling height—I finally recog-nized the orb that had been fluttering around inside of me as that bookstore feeling. It was inspiration. It was the potential of what *being-on-the-road* offered that pushed me to run. It was exciting, intoxicating, and I wanted it, so I chased it.

RONA's garden centre was another example of potential manifested. Here was this lush green oasis, within a gravelly sea of concrete, in a dull prairie suburb. I walked around it in a daze, touching the plants, smelling the flowers and getting spritzed by the overhead misters for as long as possible. I knew I would eventually have to leave: that feeling is dangerous to pursue and maintain. One needs grey to appreciate the green—and we needed to keep driving.

Back in the van, as we pushed our way down towards Calgary, cigarette smoke started to swirl, hotboxing the vehicle. It seeped into my clothes and skin. The feeling that drove me to sprint through the store, dampened. The window framed an endless expanse of concrete and asphalt. Roads led to buildings, buildings to more roads, with nothing in between.

Once we were on the highway, ragged spring grasses began to lift their little fingers from the ditch. Teetering, naked birch trees shivered in the wind. Deer watched traffic from behind the barbed wire fence of a bare canola field, keeping a safe distance from us speeding animals. Then without warning, they ran. Leaping through the dirt at odd angles, chasing or escaping something familiar and unseen.

LASER QUIT SMOKING MASSAGE

THE HOUSES ON THIS street aren't just houses. The casual observer will note that, yes, like most homes in this Saskatoon neighbourhood, they have creaking screen doors, front lawns with patchy brown grass yawning green with spring, and probably a rec room in the basement with one of those little plastic basketball nets pasted above the door frame. But the careful observer will read the signs to get a fuller understanding of what these places really are. Like, literally, read the signs. Small, square, and colourful, they speckle the stoops and windows of residences for nearly an entire city block. Bold, all caps, sans-serif type sitting on neon oranges, yellows, and greens, declaring things like:

NAILS!
MANICURE!
PEDICURE!

GREG'S TOP QUALITY
LAWN MAINTENANCE
SERVICES INC.!

WE MAKE:
SAUSAGE!
STEAKS!
JERKY!

IT'S TAX SEASON!!
DON'T WAIT!!
WE CAN HELP!!!

These houses serve as storefronts, genuine home offices, abattoir abodes, tax (agent) shelters—places I'd prefer to bring my business to. Screw the stuffy, sterile furnishings of an H&R Block; I want to go to Susan's house, hand over my T4s, and kick back with my feet on the paisley ottoman that used to belong to her great-grandmother, Delores.

There's just an added comfort and a certain type of intimacy in getting your nails done in someone's home instead of a studio. You can scan family photos on their mantel, pour yourself a glass of water from the kitchen faucet, use their personal bathroom. Maybe they're an *Uncle John's Bathroom Reader* family? I love collecting fun factoids about long-deceased hockey players while moving my bowels.

Someone inviting you into their home, even if it's for a business transaction, conveys a serious level of trust—you're entering the place where they eat, sleep and make love. That's big. When I was growing up and times got tough, my mom had to move her business, coincidentally a sign-making shop, into our basement. That meant gruff, old rural Albertan men looking for decals to splash over their semi-trucks would routinely see me in my pyjamas, drinking chocolate milk at 9 AM, while my Spider-Man action figure tried to convince Wolverine that it was okay to be sad every once and awhile. That may not seem like the optimal business environment, but the casualness helped us foster real relationships with those customers. They became like a branch of the family that had to pay us each time they came over—which is maybe how family should work, sometimes.

I don't know why the people living in this strip of houses in Saskatoon decided to bring their work lives home, but I'd surmise that not all of them did it by choice. After Alberta's economy started its free-fall in 2015, a sobering amount of people in my father's Grande Prairie neighbourhood lost their jobs, my dad barely clinging on to his own. His neighbours had all worked in the energy industry, and as that sector atrophied to the point where their individual income streams dried up, they came together to start their own mini-industry out of their homes.

They pooled resources, leased a small fleet of vehicles, and offered the city something it was missing: a late-night designated driver service. And they made pretty good bank, because even (or especially) in the face of economic collapse, people love to drink.

Maybe something similar had happened here. It could've started at a block party, where over light beer, chips and dip, the folks who live on this street expressed how expensive their storefronts were becoming, and how the inflated rent, taxes and stagnant wages were pushing them to the brink—but what could they do? The world was a merciless capitalist treadmill and the legs of their small businesses were getting tired. Perhaps that's when another neighbour suggested, jokingly at first, that to save money they should all run their businesses out of their homes, like a residential strip mall. Ha ha. That also could've been when everyone chewed that idea over privately in their heads: gauged the feasibility, the pros and cons swirling around like the chips and dip in their mouths, before realizing that this was a pretty tasty idea.

That would explain the signs: their consistent aesthetic, the same earnest, urgent messaging. They clearly all went to the same sign shop—I would know. This group also included a house at the end of the block whose sign I had to Google to figure out exactly what kind of service was being provided. When I first saw the sign, its words just didn't compute. They were a jumbled, jarring word salad. Like someone had chopped up the subject lines of all of my spam emails, put them into a hat, and plucked out four all-caps words at random:

LASER QUIT
SMOKING MASSAGE

After a few troubled minutes of trying and failing to piece together what a LASER QUIT SMOKING MASSAGE could be, I gave up; however, that quick Google search revealed that it is a technique similar to acupuncture, except with lasers that you shoot into various parts of your face—which helps you to quit smoking. Obviously.

I imagined what it would've been like as a kid, if instead of bringing the sign shop home, my mom had been a laser masseuse, watching clients come into our house, take off their shoes, and hang their jackets in the closet next to my stepdad's prized print of

Emily Carr's "Big Raven" in its tacky gold frame. My mom would get me to bring said customer a glass of iced tea as they leaned back in the recliner, taking a sip before being blasted in the face with a laser. It probably would've been pretty cool.

Running the shop out of our house wasn't any easier, though. The long hours, stress, and uncertainty my mom endured at work wouldn't stay in the basement; those feelings always slinked up the stairs, showing themselves in coldness at the dinner table or quiet tears as she smoked alone on the porch—having her source of income below her feet must have been a constant reminder that if it failed, those floorboards could come crumbling down. Were the kids in the houses on this street familiar with that same unknown pressure I had known? That pressure, which at times became overwhelming?

I wanted to know. I reached out to Saskatoon's city planning department via email and learned that it's not just 8th Street East that's turning homes into home offices. Since 2008, there's been a 72 percent increase in the number of home businesses in the city. Ellen Pearson, one of Saskatoon's senior planners, agreed with my downturn theory, saying, "I think there is a lot of truth to the general economic factors of operating out of one's home instead of renting a commercial space ..." However, there was a snag: "... but I do not have any data to provide to you to back that up."

I called the Laser Quit Smoking Massage place, but they didn't return my calls. An acupuncturist two doors down responded tersely to an email, explaining that he doesn't live out of the house itself, which seemed to be the case for a few of the places on the street. Then a local musician, who used to live around the corner from 8th East, weighed in. His financial advisor and a friend's nutrition business are on the block.

He explained that the street, a mix of commercial and residential zoning, has cheaper real estate than a traditional retail strip. He also said that, despite the recent increase, the situation still isn't unusual—that's just the way he remembers it always being.

In retrospect, I realized that was true for me, too. In a house just down the street from my childhood home in Lac La Biche was the town's only taxi service, and the family counsellor my brother and I begrudgingly saw, who practiced out of his basement. There was even a hair salon renting out my grandparents' old home just off the main drag—where, in the front yard, was the first tree I ever climbed and subsequently became traumatically stuck in, perhaps a reason for said counselling. Maybe these home storefronts were more a sign of resourcefulness and the innate ability to save a buck, each its own financial and emotional economy I'd never be privy to, no matter what I thought I saw in them. Much like how our neighbours growing up knew nothing about ours.

Further Googling informed me that the same laser techniques used to help one quit smoking could also help those struggling with depression. I thought of Wolverine and all the times I had used scraps of my mom's adhesive vinyl to bind him to chairs, walls, and the hot water tank in the basement—Logan's depressive, apathetic states often led to his capture and constraint. If I had as easy access to those lasers as I did the vinyl, maybe I could've done something for him: shot a few lasers into his grimacing plastic face, steadied his mood, helped him keep positive and out of the clutches of Shredder and the Foot Clan.

And maybe I could've turned that laser around on myself, my brother, and my mom. And maybe when things did eventually crumble, it would've kept us from the heartbreak that followed. Or, at the very least, kept us from smoking.

UNCLE FESTER

"HUGE, ROTTEN, RARE," a banner beside the entrance of the Bloedel Conservatory read. A line of hundreds snaked its way around the grounds, waiting to smell the alien-like being that had been morbidly marketed around the city all month: audio, print, and web ads all indulging in nature's gross-out sense of evolutionary humour. The why, how, and yuck of the *Amorphophallus titanum*. Titan arum. The corpse flower. A rare Indonesian plant that smells like dead shit.

Every seven to ten years, this hulking thing blossoms, its spathe opening like the soft verdant hand of a giant presenting a pungent gift. However, the gift is a trap. To the insect world, the smell of decomposing meat is what high school boys imagine the scent of Calvin Klein cologne to be—pure allure. Beetles and flies make their way into the flower, luxuriating in its putridness.

The plant remains open for only a few short hours before closing in on itself and the bugs. Trapped, the bugs are forced to wander inside the grasp of the corpse flower, caking themselves in its pollen until it releases its grip. Eventually, its one large petal will peel back, freeing the insects, who then go about their lives, unwitting pollinators for one of nature's smelliest flora.

At the conservatory, The Beatles' "All You Need is Love" blared over the loudspeakers as part of a hokey mash of love songs meant to intimate that, yes, the corpse flower was trying to *reproduce*. To *make love* with the earth. A fact that once realized made me a bit uncomfortable. We were a line of voyeurs all waiting to watch this thing fuck in its own complicated way. A few paces ahead, a trio of elderly Ukrainian women deliberated on whether the wait would be worth it, asking a volunteer (whose shirt was emblazoned with an all-caps "WHAT'S THAT SMELL?") how long it would take.

"Whaaaa!" The smallest of the three gasped. They huddled and muttered amongst themselves, measuring their interest in consensually smelling the fetid plant against the two hours it would take to reach it. The sun pushed down on them with heavy hands as they calculated. They were still at least forty-five minutes away from even making it to the section of the line covered by a row of collapsible tents—shade the most valuable of real estate here.

The smallest of the women threw her hands into the air in defeat; another took one last look at the line and capitulated. The third decided to stay, beaming as she waved goodbye to her friends: The smell was an experience she would have earned, that she could hold over them, an exercise in endurance and curiosity.

An hour from the entrance to the building, a couple started furiously swiping through their phones.

"We can make it, right?"

"Yeah, I mean. One hour? We get in, see the thing, run out, get a taxi."

"Are there any later flights? Can we swap tickets or anything?"

He made a phone call. This couple was so dedicated to whatever olfactory rush they thought they were in for that they were willing to miss their flight back to Los Angeles. I wanted to ask them why. Was the prospect of this stench that appealing? I bounced back and forth between their eager faces. Are there not things that smell this terrible in California? I remember floating along the water track of "It's a Small World" at Disneyland as a child, watching the soulless animatronic children singing about unity or whatever, and being completely distracted by the smell that lifted itself from the waterway and entered our nostrils. It was that of damp clothing, the rank armpits of a coffee drinker, and blood.

Still, I had let my fingers drag over the water's surface, losing sight of the ripples behind us as we entered the black of the tunnel. My hand tingled. It became clear that my flesh would be eaten away by whatever bacteria or curse had been cast on the river by the ride's possessed animatronic children and their squealing hinges. I sat on my hand for the rest of the ride, praying I would be okay, trying to ignore the smell. The feeling. That had to have been worse than whatever the corpse flower would offer.

As we finally neared the entrance, the Ukrainian woman and I grinned at one another. It was a reason to celebrate and bare teeth. I smiled as a sunburn stung the back of my neck and arms like a hard slap. I hadn't made it to the tent section in time to save my skin.

A person from the botanical garden with a parrot on their arm ambled down the line toward us. Along with the occasional bottle of water and ETA update, this was an attempt to keep the garden's patrons happy. The bird's name was Blanca. Its off-white feathers bristled as the man displayed it for all of the scorched, weary waiters.

"Say hello to all of the nice folks," he encouraged. Blanca ducked its head under a wing and let out a low squawk, expressing its embarrassment for all of us in the line-up.

The couple from Los Angeles cooed, talked to the bird as though it were a small human child and told her—despite Blanca not interacting with us, and giving us some heavy side-eye—that she was a good girl. *A geeeewwwwd gyuuuuuuugrl.* "She's just tired," her handler told us, trying to assuage whatever worries he thought we had, as if our egos would be bruised. Why should we expect this creature, stuck in captivity, to want to interact with us? I wondered if any of the botanical garden's patrons had ever taught Blanca curse words, as she stared at the Ukrainian woman through parted wingtips. The woman glared back. This was the kind of interaction I was interested in—interspecies skepticism.

Once inside, it took little time to reach the corpse flower. A steady procession shuffled through the conservatory, past rare Australian bushes and invasive Brazilian grasses, while other parrots with names like Rudy and Nelson wailed around them.

Everything living under the building's large glass dome had been given a name, even the corpse flower. The plant's moniker was decided by a public vote, and as we got closer to it—the main event, the grand stink, what the weirdly targeted ads in my social media feeds had been spinning all week, the reason we were all here—a small placard revealed its democratically given title: Uncle Fester.

Uncle Fester was bigger and more phallic than I had imagined. Its engorged spadix pointed proudly, boastfully, towards the ceiling. However, we were told that in a few days, it would wilt, and become dramatically unimpressive. Comically flaccid. But in the waning hours, thousands of people would gawk in awe at its turgidity.

Unfortunately, that's all they'd be taking in, because as we finally got in front of it, taking in its physical presence, that's all there was. No one was holding their nose. Not a single person gagged with the sick delight of someone who had spent a quarter of their day waiting to do just that.

A reporter from CTV scribbled in his notebook, making last-minute amendments as his camera operator did their best to frame him so that the corpse flower sat prominently over his left shoulder. Another parrot brought attention to itself with a yelp as a light on the camera blinked red.

"Well, this isn't what most had hoped for. The smell of the Titan arum—that of rotten meat—has drawn a crowd of hundreds today; but that stench has, unfortunately, passed."

The Ukrainian woman, her grin gone, followed the perimeter of the area roped off for the corpse flower, stopping to point her nose in the air. Hungry for just a whiff, something to bring back to her friends, to justify her staying. Blanca screamed from her perch like a car alarm. We could all read between the lines:

Y'all been had, y'all been had, y'all been had.

THE DARK LORD OF VANCOUVER KARAOKE

ARCANABYSS CORVGOTH'S BLACK LEATHER trench coat pools on the floor around the chair he's sitting on. The crisscrossing of metal chains at his waist hangs over the edge of the seat, and studded armbands glint under the soft, recessed lights of 12 Kings Pub. Well over six feet tall and clad in all-black garb with only his face visible from under his hood, Arcanabyss sticks out like a pallid, vampiric thumb in a room that looks like the results you'd get from Google Image searching the keywords "sports," "bar," "bro," and "testosterone." But only the uninitiated would think he didn't belong here.

At 12 Kings, Arcanabyss reigns. Especially on Saturdays, because today is the Lord's Day. And what the uninitiated don't realize as his statuesque form rises and makes its way to the microphone—where a DJ has queued up Judas Priest's "Victim of Changes," its lyrics about to scroll down the large flat screen mounted on the wall behind them —is that Arcanabyss Corvgoth is the Dark Lord of Vancouver Karaoke.

* * *

"Knightly obeisances, sire," Arcanabyss says as a big mitt emerges from his trench coat, enveloping my own. Around us is chaos. The Tim Hortons he's chosen to meet at, somewhere in the heart of Richmond, BC, is teeming with cooing, crying babies, gossiping elderly folks, and kids glued to their cellphones. It is a surprisingly raucous scene. One that I didn't expect from how Arcanabyss pitched it to me while setting up our interview:

"I concurrence chummy confabulation at sanctum of palatable pastries, Tim Hortons, afternoontide of 4 PM? It stands coterminous to conveyance structurum 'Richmond Brighouse' station."

The first time I spoke with Arcanabyss, after having a few too many ciders while at 12 Kings karaoke some months previous, I had no idea what he was saying. He speaks in his own dialect, one that sounds like a combination of Old English and a bespoke high-fantasy tongue. Or, as he describes it on his Facebook "about" page, "I am a grammarian fluent in anachronistic elocution, because I bestow ardent logolatry for words."

That logolatry is hard to decode at first. The regality of his speech conjures images that don't always fit with our current time—this Tim Hortons feeling more like a New York City bus depot than a "sanctum of palatable pastries." But once you sit in front of him for a few minutes and see the words leave his sharp, slender face, it's easier to understand; and it even becomes jarring when he occasionally has to break out of his "anachronistic elocution" to communicate certain things, such as his order: "Umm, I'll just have an Iced Capp. Thanks."

However, when he sings it doesn't feel like a departure from his chosen style of speech. Even when Rob Halford's deftly poetic lyrics like "You 'bin fooling' with some hot guy" come out of

Arcanabyss' mouth, it feels on-brand. His ability to hit notes within an operatic range is compelling in a way that is hard to explain. Singing is a self-taught skill, or as his business card—which he gave to me on my cidery first encounter with him—states, he is a "self-mastered countertenor/male" in the genre of "heavy metal/power metal."

After he finishes his first song of the evening, the crowd at 12 Kings erupts. There is even a short-lived chant of his name. Here at karaoke night, Arcanabyss is beyond mortal. There are people here just to see him sing. And when the DJ announces that tonight is, in fact, the Dark Lord's birthday, a second, louder round of cheers and hoots roll through the bar. Back at his table, which is full of 20 to 30 friends and family (or, as he puts it, "effervescent comradeships/sectators of mine"), he has trouble connecting with all the awaiting high-fives.

Next up to the mic is Arcanabyss' mom, who dedicates Metallica's "Enter Sandman" to her son. It is strange and touching. Her guttural Hetfield flourishes are surprisingly affecting.

"Love yah, sweetie," she says into the mic as the final guitar riff fades. His mother was responsible for bringing Arcanabyss to his first karaoke night, seven years ago, at a nondescript joint in Surrey, BC. This experience eventually snowballed into his passion, one that started with him singing along to classic songs in Disney "paragons" like *Aladdin* and *The Lion King*, then meandering into bands like Scorpions, then Bowie, until heavy metal became his foundation.

He refers to singing karaoke as an "unveiling." While he does literally pull his hood from his face before each performance, he is referring to a deeper personal reveal. On stage he gets to be himself for everyone to see—and they very much want to bear witness. This is something that he was never afforded earlier in life. He adopted his style of speech and dress at eight years old, and for the simple transgression of being himself, he suffered severe bullying in school. To now draw crowds like this on a weekly basis and have an entire bar wish you a happy birthday must feel like validation—a victory of sorts.

Karaoke has also given Arcanabyss a community. Beyond his fans, he's cultivated friendships, which include Cowboy Dan: a slight, middle-aged crooner in a Stetson who has become a brother to him. They have a "domicile allegiance" out in Richmond, and drive Dan's "shimmerous steed" out to various karaoke nights around the Lower Mainland.

Arcanabyss has manifested this all for himself. By remaining unabashedly who he wants to be, a world suited to his ideals eventually formed around him—the scene in 12 Kings full of similar magical conjurings. Cowboy Dan leads the entire bar in a rendition of "I'm Gonna Be (500 Miles)" by The Proclaimers, each person singing along as though genuinely declaring their love and the lengths they'd go to fulfill it. A barrel-chested man screams Christina Aguilera's "Genie in A Bottle" into the microphone, spittle flecking his chest-length beard, in what becomes one of the most entertaining performances of the night.

Then a young woman waits for the lyrics to Jay-Z and Kanye's "N****s in Paris" to appear on screen, which they never do. As the song starts, she implores the DJ to find a version of the song with lyrics, but all he does is look at her and mouth, "That shit cray." She stutters and it appears as though she's about to crumble until something sparks, and as if possessed, the words start flowing out of her. The crowd cheers and dances—until she, a white woman, raps the n-word and the collective whiteness of the bar cringes back into its seats.

That's the overwhelming power—and danger—of karaoke. Over the course of a song, you are allowed to become whomever you want to be. To tell stories that aren't yours, which is not always a good thing. But for Arcanabyss, the magic of karaoke is merely an extension of his own story. An outlet for his ability and the persona he's built around it. When I ask him about his name, he gives me an equation:

Arcane = Mystery

Abyss = Eternal Blackness

Arcane + Abyss = Arcanabyss

He is the mystery of eternal blackness. He chose his moniker as a tribute to how the world has misinterpreted him—to spite that world. He could never imagine conforming, speaking in the stunted "platitudes" of the "ultra-modernists" who text around us in the Tim Hortons. That's why he speaks with a "resplendent flow" inspired by HP Lovecraft and Edgar Allan Poe. His pop idol is Cthulhu. Arcanabyss is the figurehead of his own cult at 12 Kings.

✳ ✳ ✳

From across the table, Arcanabyss' mother pushes a gift into his hands.

"We got you something. Open it."

He does, in silence.

"It's a wind chime," she explains. "You can put it up somewhere around your place, by a window or something, and it'll make noise."

Silence.

"Did you see what it says on it? 'Be The Change.'"

This moment, overheard by a friend before I arrived on Arcanabyss' birthday night, is fitting if not paradoxically apt. Like most people, I initially learned about the Dark Lord of Vancouver Karaoke second-hand. At first, via small details from a friend describing the sight and the atmosphere he creates, then by an Instagram video shared with glee. When I saw him in person, I was taken aback by his passion for his craft. His full-throated, self-mastered, countertenor commitment. Now I regularly go to karaoke night with my friends, something we never did before, and we have a great goddamn time. That's because of Arcanabyss.

So, he has been the change by simply not changing for others at all.

THE BIG DOG IN THE SKY IS DIRTY

On a pedestal 25 feet in the air, it looks blankly over the crook of Main St. and 18th Ave. Its unblinking eyes fixed toward the north have been collecting dust and muck kicked up from southward Vancouver traffic for over a decade. The backside of the 7-foot aluminum poodle is pristine, as though confirming that facing the present head-on, unobstructed, day in and day out, is an unhealthy proposition.

Untitled (*Poodle*) is the work of Gisele Amantea, a Calgary-born and Montréal-based artist. Commissioned as a public art project by the City of Vancouver, it cost $97,600 to create and erect in January 2013. Amantea's artist statement reads vaguely, "[*Untitled* (*Poodle*)] is intended as a curiosity that will attract attention to [the sculpture] as a marker or icon of time and place."

In a way, this intention was met. For a time, *Untitled* (*Poodle*) was an icon of its place, 3333 Main St. It inspired hot takes, lukewarm takes ("I Kinda Like Vancouver's New Poodle In The Sky" read one *VICE* headline at the time), and also @MainStPoodle: a deeply uninspired Twitter account that would tweet things in the voice of the poodle like "Received a Valentine's card from a 'secret admirer.' Really hope it's not a cat," and "Apologies for the wet dog smell pervading Main Street. I need an umbrella. #Raincouver"

The sculpture was decried as a marker of the city's ignorance of the neighbourhood's rampant gentrification: this fancy toy dog installed in front of an expensive new condominium development in a city whose housing crisis has been doing nothing but escalate. In response, a local sculptor and geocacher installed a series of concrete turds at its base. One coiler was painted a classic deep brown, another a glittering gold.

But mostly, *Untitled (Poodle)* has been forgotten. Up on its perch for over ten years, the dog has become simply a bauble, an easy-to-miss ornament, a thing to notice if you happen to look up. The interest it arrived with petered out quickly, the @MainStPoodle Twitter account mercifully running out of juice in February 2015.

"Not associated with a particular culture, [the poodle] can be appreciated by the wide range of people along the street and in the surrounding neighbourhoods," Amantea said in her artist's statement, a banal sentiment that also serves as an effective credo for most city-sanctioned public art, where a work's aesthetic value is directly tied to how broad and bland its appeal is, lest it offends the sensibility of the passerby, but more importantly, the property owner.

In the summer of 2021, Chinese artist Chen Wenling's sculpture *Boy Holding A Shark* was set to be installed in Vancouver's waterfront neighbourhood of False Creek as a part of the Vancouver International Sculpture Biennale: a city-wide, open-air public art exhibition. The nearly 26-foot-tall piece depicts a distressed young boy cradling a melting shark in his arms. The Vancouver Biennale website describes Wenling's sculpture as "the artist's reflection on the growing tension between humans and the ocean. It is an alert that the destruction of nature will eventually counteract humanity itself. The artist hopes to evoke concerns about environmental issues through the power of art and inspire changes in the global community."

Wenling's sculpture, at that point just a digital mockup, spurred more than 1,500 people to sign an online petition to stop the sculpture's installation. "It will obscure views, which will affect property values and sell-ability," one signatory wrote in the petition's comments. "The statue evoked fear, disgust, and unease in me ... It is a horrifying vision to behold," wrote another. The City ultimately capitulated to the disgusted and horrified; *Boy Holding A Shark* would not find a home in False Creek. Or anywhere, as of writing this. The petition's organizer revelled in the success while gearing up for a future battle.

"Great News is that Vancouver Public Art has now stated that the Sculpture will not be located in this location and a new location is is [sic] to be selected. Where will this new location be? We have succeeded for now?" The group had self-appointed themselves as guardians against "horrifying visions" no matter what neighbourhood they may reside in. Perhaps if the boy and the shark were not deep in stages of grief and decomposition, the piece would've had a better chance to "be appreciated by the wide range of people along the street and in the surrounding neighbourhoods." The artist's dire message of ecological collapse free to amass dirt, dust and seagull guano if its subject would just put a little smile on.

Which led me to wonder, if public art like this is so divisive and damaging to citizens and their property values, why wasn't anyone cleaning the safe, sterile, and condominium-approved seven-foot-tall poodle in the sky? Couldn't someone give the big dog a little scrub? Wash the gunk from its eyes and the muck caking its paws.

` When I first noticed the dirty dog in early February 2022, I emailed the City of Vancouver and asked why *Untitled (Poodle)* had remained in such a state for so long. I received a swift and kind response explaining that the process of getting permits for lifts and lane closures to safely secure the space and equipment required to bathe the faux-porcelain pooch was an arduous one. But hopefully, by March, the sculpture would be fresh and sparkling in the first rays of the spring sun. Two days later, it was clean. Only once had I seen the city act with more haste when it came to public art.

In the early hours of the morning on September 9, 2014, a nine-foot-tall statue of a buck-naked all-red devil with large black horns and an enormous erection was installed at Clark Drive near 4th Avenue in a long-disused public square that used to be home to a bronze bust of Christopher Columbus. "Penis Satan," as it came to be known, the project of an anonymous artist who goes by the name "Obsidian," was removed before the workday was through. Speaking to CTV News, Ammar Mahimwalla, a former project manager for the Vancouver International Sculpture Biennale, praised their work, saying it was well-made and well-installed; however, "With the city, sometimes, there is censorship—at some level—of what art means and what art is." Which, in this instance, I guess makes sense. Having to pass Lucifer's giant red cock on your morning commute may not be for everyone. But despite, and perhaps thanks to its crude nature, "Penis Satan" has been one of the most popular pieces of public art Vancouver has known in recent memory. Its existence a direct—and successful—response to the city's deeply ingrained prudishness.

Untitled (Poodle), it appeared, was the city's ideal public artwork—something so benign and out of the way that it could be completely forgotten about, yet attended to with ease on the off chance that someone does remember it. Because, as the city would seem to tell us, what is art if not glorified set dressing? Why would you want to add any undue pressure on the vast twisting cogs of bureaucracy, do anything but *increase* perceived property values, or risk any greater conversation around art beyond its own obsequiousness intent—much like "Spinning Chandelier," a 26' tall crystal chandelier installation by the late Vancouver artist Rodney Graham, did. Initially commissioned by the developer Westbank for 1.2 million in 2019 with its final price tag rising to 4.8 million dollars, it spins underneath the Granville Bridge in the shadow of Vancouver House, a luxury skyscraper developed by Westbank. At the time, the installation was similarly decried as an oblivious extravagance and affront to the city's increasing housing and homelessness crisis. I wonder now if most people fail to look up.

Gilded dookies can be tossed into the garbage, grime can be pressure-washed away. In Vancouver, a city hellbent on maintaining an ever-worsening status quo, there will always be time for solutions that give meaningful attention to the meaningless. It's perhaps telling that even then, they forgot to take care of their lapdog.

MAGIC

It's called a Brooklyn Arctic Adventure but you're not *in* Brooklyn. Well, technically, you are. City Point BKLYN, the shopping mall where the virtual reality Arctic Adventure pop-up is happening, is right in the borough's downtown core. But once you sit in the plush chair and have the attendant tighten the VR gear onto your head—you're in the North Pole.

A snowman shuffles towards you and offers a welcome. Its voice soft and kind. It lets you in on a little secret: Santa has personally invited you to his workshop. The sole reindeer pulling the sleigh you have no choice but to sit in takes off running through a village of brownstones, polar bears, and SUVs that comically peel out into the snow. I disorientate myself by craning my neck from one side to another in the chair. I want to know this world from all angles. Get a peek into its inhabitants' day-to-day. Listen for the community's heartbeat and watch how the community ambles along—every small town has its gait. And, most pressingly, how does the holiday season translate into this choppy virtual reality?

The reindeer is hauling ass. I'm unable to take in everything the city has to offer before the sleigh leaves the ground, and without tipping the chair as my IRL self is swivelling. Birds are racing us in the perfect blue of the sky. I reach out to touch them but see nothing where my hands should be. When we land in Santa's compound, a line of jigging elves has cordoned off the Gingerbread Village. This likely wasn't meant to appear malicious, but their kicks look dangerous and deliberate. As with Muay Thai, the choreographed elbows and knees swing with intent.

As if startled by the display, the sleigh makes a hard left and worms its way inside Santa's workshop—reindeer hooves clomping on the carpet. Santa meets us in the lobby. His smooth, bulbous features move awkwardly and out of sync with his words as he tells me I've been a good child and asks what I want for Christmas. During his expectant pause I tell him nothing. My desires are my own. I do not require help to attain them.

Behind Kris is a detailed, lifelike portrait of what one would assume is Mrs. Claus. Some online sources claim her name to be anything from Jessica to Gertrude to Carol. She appears to be a different species than her shining Pixar'd husband. She looks down warmly on all of us.

Santa shoos us away and we move into the workshop itself. Inside, table after table of elves pound unidentifiable tools into little dinosaurs, action figures, and brightly-coloured Rubik's Cubes. Toys of a different era, the only thing placing them in the now are the elves' smartphones resting on the worktables. One elf checks their notifications before returning to stick tiny pokey spines into cutesy little Stegosauruses.

The elves don't look up, their shoulders slouched. No eye contact. How long are their workdays? Do they receive benefits? One table off in the corner is shrouded in darkness. The only light coming from it are the phones scattered across the workstation. Was this a punishment? Are you relegated to the shadow table if you don't meet the daily quota? No explanation is given before your reindeer books it out the door. In the hallway, a pair of elves dance in front of a row of machines that pump out jack-in-the-boxes, bouncy balls and rocking horses. A distraction from the deep sorrow of the previous room.

Back in the lobby, Santa tells you the show's over, thanks you for coming, and asks you to visit the website of the VR company that has brought you here as your sleigh rips out of the workshop and back into the snow, where you rise into the blue once more, mountains crystalline in the distance. The feeling of flight offered is a shoddy but serviceable replication. The stomach flutters at takeoff and when the sleigh takes hard lateral swings, even though the brain is aware of the trickery at hand. Santa's compound shrinks below, this reality a pleasant interpretation of a fabrication that has been tradition for generations.

✳ ✳ ✳

Stop pushing. Don't you push me again. Goddamit, stop shoving, shouted to the instrumental tune of "Jingle Bells" permeating 5th Ave. These are the refrains ringing out from the crowd. The sidewalk packed tight, hot, and moist like meatloaf in a tray. Pedestrian traffic has been at a standstill for nearly twenty minutes. Thousands of people are waiting for and watching the Saks Fifth Avenue light display. A halogen castle lights up on the building's facade. Bright colours burst and bleed as a corny carol I can't place is dumped into the air by speakers from somewhere. Everywhere. The crowd *oohs, ahhs* and *ah fuck get outta my ways.*

Some, like me, have made the mistake of coming this route and are now trapped. Others are *really* here for it. Clapping and hooting as the lights flash. Giving it up for that old-fashioned commodified Christmas spirit. I'm not innocent, though. I'm here for the tree at Rockefeller Center. It takes nearly a half hour of waiting and worming through the crowd to reach it. This whole ordeal, which has become traumatic in a particularly festive way, is part of a plan.

I will take a photo of the tree and send it to my family, with a tongue-in-cheek caption calling the glowing green giant "inferior" and "amateurish" compared to Ladysmith, BC's annual Christmas tree light-up: a past tradition of ours in which we watched a modest conifer, decorated loosely around its base with lights, get turned on. Most of the town makes it out for the event, their faces glowing with artificial light.

I don't make it past the metal barrier on 50th St. From that vantage, I take a quick snap with my phone of the 72-foot tall Norway Spruce and head to the subway. This staple holiday tradition is gruelling, humanity-draining, but accomplished. Back in Brooklyn, I walk. The sidewalks are spacious. I amble from one side to the other, taking full advantage of the freedom. A pickup truck speeds past; in the box is a giant menorah lit by Christmas lights cutting through the night.

A series of RVs roar by. Sticking out of the small rear windows are the heads of yarmulke-wearing children screaming and laughing, wishing me a happy Hanukkah. Duct-taped to the sides of the RVs are pieces of cardboard with large Sharpie letters declaring the vehicles "Mitzvah tanks": Mobile outposts for Orthodox Jews trying to reach non-believers and those within the faith who've lost their way. "Mini-synagogues" on wheels. Rolling temple.

Kids screech with glee. *"Haaaaaaappppppyyyy Hannnuuuuk-kaaaahhhh!"* I wave and wish them one back as Mitzvah tanks roll by like a military parade. These caravans have been making their way through New York City streets since the '70s. Now the tanks have their own YouTube channels with series like "Judaism on the Go" and Twitter accounts that retweet Buzzfeed listicles. Traditions evolve. Practices adapt.

Along Bushwick Ave., Jesus holds his ground. Attached to the front of an apartment, encased in glass, is a nearly life-sized sculpture of the Virgin Mary kneeling in prayer. I stop to take a photo but pull back as an elderly woman emerges from the building. Small, stoic, and with recycling. She smiles and I smile back and continue walking. A block down, a nondescript brick church is outfitted with a digital display that looks like a high school gymnasium scoreboard. Dull orange pixels splash across it, a message in five parts, fully animated.

JESUS (transition to crashing waves)

IS THE (transition to blooming flowers)

REASON (transition to hands steepled in prayer)

FOR THE (transition to wisemen walking across desert, guiding star in far-right corner)

SEASON (transition to fireworks. Big, booming.)

Back in my Airbnb, I watch a rain gutter swing in front of my bedroom window. It had fallen the night before and now hangs there, pushed like a pendulum by the wind. Sometimes the wind holds strong, leaving the gutter to pause at one side of the window longer than the other, teasing a return. It's mesmerizing. I watch it while eating potato chips. Crumbs dust my bare chest like sugar. Who is responsible for this magic? The gutter swings back, stops halfway, and returns from where it came.

ONLINE & FOREVER

PINK FIELD

AGE OF EMPIRES II is the popular sequel to the iconic historical, real-time strategy video game *Age of Empires* (clearly). In it, you can role-play as Byzantine Romans, Celts, Mongols, Turks, and many more once-dominant civilizations that now live up to their former glories only in digital, playable form. The goal is to build an empire (obviously), which means harvesting natural resources, developing an army, and then conquering your neighbours in true Stone to Modern Age fashion.

I don't play to annex and destroy, though. I play to landscape. The map editor mode allows the player to create their own simulated geographies from scratch. You can run rivers through farmlands, establish a humble fishing village, or form mountain ranges and choose from fir, pine, bamboo or broad leafy maple trees to dress their towering ridges.

Deep in a valley I authored, thick with forest, I squeezed in a meadow of tall grass, invisible to all but those in it. Deer and wild sheep grazed, colourful birds sang overhead. There was peace there. A narrow path led from the meadow, winding slow and long through the trees, dappled sunlight dressing a lone curious lamb as it made its way towards a pond at the path's end. A crystalline blue pool of rippling pixels was made shallow at its edges so animals could soak, before it dropped sharply into a murky dark. Water has to be a certain depth before the map editor mode allows one to place fish—salmon and tuna leapt and splashed, confined and contented to swim small circles around their fairytale home.

Scroll north of the pond and you reach the riverbank. Ambient music from some online mix open in a separate tab, hummed, blipped, and chirped while I carved the river through the pixels of this place. Mountains and trees disappeared, stepped on and pushed out of existence as my cursor clicked. I divided the map into sections with more blue flowing ribbons—small tributaries like fingers touching the live wire of the main river.

I was more instinct than thought when creating this world. My body sunk into the couch, hours became both fluid and ignored. Dark winter nights would end at 4 AM with me lost in a great ocean, populating it with swordfish and sandbars. Some nights I would build entire cities: expansive neighbourhoods where people played, traded wares at the market, or came home from the gold mine each evening to their families.

Only once did I design a war: a battle between two communities divided by a creek, a small bridge the only means of reaching either side. There was a whole rise-of-fascism subplot I kept track of in my head—inspired by the news of the day. It was incumbent upon the Persians to squash the insidious brand of hate that was boiling over with the neighbouring Britons. Provoked by attacks on Persian lumber mills and the murder of a trade merchant, we were forced to take action. Persian cannoneers blew apart the Britons' gates and took down their armoury. Their archers, long swordsmen, and vague historical figures on horseback with boosted hit-points tried to defend against our onslaught but were no match. Even civilians attempted to fend us off, but our war elephants trampled them and walked right through their homes, where their families slept. Our army streamed towards their castle and, within minutes, tore it down, which granted us victory. Rubble and blurry bodies of the mutilated all around.

That night I went to bed at 4 AM again, uneasy. I didn't want to devote hours to a massacre, to building an *empire*. I wanted to bring beauty to this world. A memory floated into view. A visit to Toronto and June Callwood Park, strolling over its pink ground under the shade of trees. A novel, contemporary interpretation of public space and something that seemed like it would be more enjoyable to create than the predetermined slaughtering of an enemy's army. I grabbed my phone from the bedside table and looked up the designer of June Callwood Park, Pat Hanson.

I'd learn that the park was inspired by a quote taken from the last interview acclaimed journalist and activist June Callwood gave before her death in 2007:

"I believe in kindness."

Hanson and her team turned that quote into a physical design, the park itself shaped by the audio frequency of Callwood's words: the mix of dull grey and bright candy pink concrete strips of walkway within it representing June's actual vocal wave pattern.

The park starts at Fort York Boulevard, where, viewed from above, concrete strips peak at the vocal wave's "I" in Callwood's quote, receding briefly before bursting with a flourish of pink during "believe," ebbing until the park becomes raucous with colour and concrete as the pink slabs dance up and down the park "in kindness," the words "echoing" permanently across almost an entire city block. The spaces Callwood's words don't fill, the silences, are packed with dark soil. Small, leafy trees placed throughout. It's a surreal thing to walk in a forest whose floor is mostly Pepto Bismol-coloured cement and benches.

I had moved slowly through the park, which is divided into different sections. Each has a name that would fit better in Middle Earth than it does squished awkwardly between Gzowski Boulevard and Bastion Street. A gaggle of teenagers with phones in front of their faces posed on blocks in the *Puzzle Garden*; two suited men with coffee in their hands talked loudly to one another about numbers with name designations I did not understand in the middle of *Puddle Plaza*; two beagles hurried in tandem to keep up with their owner through the *Pink Field*, their little legs skipping across the ground in a blur; the *Time Strip Gardens* were the biggest and loudest portions of the park, with large shifting groups of people shuffling under the trees, their voices mixing and converging in a live sound experiment — a ransom note comprised of errant words from private conversations.

The sentence and park end with the *Ephemeral Pools*, where lustered jets push water into the air. The actual "pools" are haphazardly placed, their waters seeping into the cracks between the concrete planks on the ground, feeding the weeds that have slowly crawled through, green fingertips prying. A feeling of peace, tentative but tangible, wormed its warmth through my body as I arrived at Fleet Street—the park's punctuation.

I try to recreate that sensation in my *Age of Empires II* map editor mode, clicking my cursor in a steady, hypnotic rhythm as I trace the candy-corn-shaped outline of the park. There is no appropriately pink-coloured terrain to put down for the *Pink*

Field, so I have to work with what I've got. An arid desert sand is the best available option. The classic leafy maple tree selection works perfectly, though, and the grid pattern that the editor system operates with suits my emulation perfectly as I plop each tree into a square plot of soil. There are even little fountains that spurt in homage to the *Ephemeral Pools*.

It takes two shifts to finish construction on my personal Callwood Park. 4 AM bold in the top corner of my computer screen each night. However, once it's done, it just sits empty. Hollow. It was clear that feeling I was chasing wasn't just contingent on the concrete element but the human, too.

I fill the park with villagers from every civilization, their colourful tunics popping on the grey stone and sandy ground. But after I finish populating the park, the people only stand and sway in *Puddle Plaza* and make no designs to navigate *The Maze*. They are waiting for my command, for the simulation to start. I hesitate because I will lose control of their actions once it begins. The AI that drives them is practical and cruel. Harvest, build, kill. Their programming is unnervingly human. That wouldn't be the tenuous feeling of contentment I wanted to fabricate and bottle within this video game.

Warily, I put the map on *Test Mode*. The villagers' voices rise from the speakers as the simulation starts. I watch them walk in small circles. Men and women in their bold tunics bumble through the *Time Strip Gardens* and cluster in the *Puzzle Garden*. Despite the goals of the game they were born into, they do not draw any weapons; they don't curse or stick with just their own—they mix, talk, and look to be enjoying the pixelated park. I watch them as a song with a faint crooning saxophone plays, providing a soundtrack to what I envision as a moment of genuine happiness in their limited digital lives. One jazzy mix leads into another from a tab open in my browser window. A taste of the feeling I was chasing from the life-sized Callwood Park worms its way back. Their peace is my peace.

A song transitions into the next, this one with a staggered, thudding beat. The villagers seem to be singing along—a chorus of Vikings and Goths and Teutons and Aztecs and Incas. I scroll over to the *Time Strip Gardens*, half hoping to see them organized into a choir, carolling, cajoling others to join in. When I find them, they're moving at a frantic pace, not singing but grunting. They're working. Hard. The thuds I thought to be part of the song are the sounds of their axes cutting down the trees in the park. I shout at them to stop but they don't listen. They carry great pieces of maple to lumber mills they've clandestinely built on the outskirts of the park. I watch, pained, as they clear each section of its greenery. They build houses in the *Ephemeral Pools*. A stable in the *Pink Field*. Sentry towers line Fleet Street.

The thudding and grunting subside once there's nothing left for their axes to strike. They wander aimlessly. Eventually, even their conversations slow until no one speaks at all. A mass of villagers forms in the *Maze*. Shoulder to shoulder. Each person just a pinch of pixels. A blur of faces looks up into the sky I occupy, waiting to know what's next.

IN THE GALAXY LIGHT OF THE MIRACLE

THE HOUSE SPARROWS that frequent the bird feeder on my balcony like to swing from it—one, two, eight of them at a time. They don't often squabble over the suet block; instead, they make space for one another even as room on the feeder grows limited. I watch them chirp and flit outside my window. They puff their feathers, preen on the railing, and share the strange, hardened mixture of fat, fruit, and bugs hanging in the cool morning air.

* * *

I first noticed it in the comment section. Professional Skateboarder A.) would post a video of a skateboarding trick to Instagram, and Professional Skateboarder B.) would shoot off a short, enthusiastic response. In the case of pro skater Andrew Brophy, his usual exclamation was a booming, all-caps "GANG!"

This isn't particularly unusual on its own, but Brophy wouldn't just comment on one post. It was all of the posts. Follow enough professional skateboarders and you'll see it take shape: every skater in every other skater's comments, leaving a trail of prayer hands and fire emojis in their wake. While supportive, positive messages are obviously not a bad thing (and should be encouraged), patterns start to emerge for those who steadily scroll their feeds: phrases that appear copy-and-pasted from one post to the next. Brophy's commenting habits were notorious enough to inspire a SLAP message board thread dedicated to collecting (and skewering) his constant exclamations at his colleagues' clips.

Now, it's known that this is part of a technique to organically grow your follower count. The more you comment, the higher the likelihood that people will see your profile, interact with it, and potentially press that "follow" button—basic online brand-building stuff, by today's standards. Cringey, yes, but not terrible. Together, the skateboarders create a self-sustaining promotional ecosystem. One that requires only a quick, gracious few taps of the keyboard as the algorithm ushers you along.

✳ ✳ ✳

There's a literal pecking order to the bird feeder on my balcony. Since the starlings are bigger and more prone to scream and attack if anyone else tries to eat beside them, the house sparrows are left to patter around on the ground, waiting for crumbs to drop from above until their turn comes. The big birds' success provides a not-insignificant hustle for the smalls if they can make it work.

✳ ✳ ✳

A photo of a skunk doing a handstand, a bloody one-sided street fight where a loudmouth is served a comeuppance, a vaguely humorous subtweet. When a Twitter post goes viral, whatever it may be, there's a high likelihood that it'll be "piggybacked" by companies looking to market their products. If you've spent enough time on Twitter, you've surely seen this in action.

A tweet from a relatively small account reaches a certain level of traction and the author of the tweet is approached by a company that offers them about $25 to tweet about their product in the same thread—exposing that product to thousands of eyes quietly wondering why a video of a man pretending to close the fridge door on his child's head is so popular. It's a vacuous, parasitic promotional strategy that, judging by the few responses these attachment tweets get, is limited in its effectiveness.

It also showcases the strange morality of a viral post. In one viral tweet reacting to another viral tweet, the first follow-up post is a link to a GoFundMe page for a transgender youth in need. The following tweets are for Galaxy Lights, an alleged weight loss technique, and a "detox mask" featuring an uncomfortably close-up video of someone getting blackheads pulled from their face.

Does the author of the secondary viral tweet bear any responsibility towards using their sudden platform to boost an urgent cause? Is that good intention undone at all by the subsequent hawking of cheap products? Is this simply another festering symptom of late-stage capitalism? Whatever the case, this tortured economy of virality continues.

✳ ✳ ✳

When the feeder gets busy, the crows take notice. They barge onto the balcony, taking the space from the starlings and sparrows. But they're far too big for the suet-block feeder, their bodies eveloping the small metal cage. Unable to hang on, they jump and dive, crashing into it in hopes of some morsel of food breaking free. It is clumsy, awkward work, and I know it's complete when I hear the feeder get knocked from its hook and crash to the ground.

✷ ✷ ✷

If something goes viral online, it's because it has some inherent initial value. Maybe it's a funny meme, a vital news story, or a video of a puppy sitting on a goose's back. It gets shared because we want others to interact with it and, in turn, interact with us. Virality always has an upper limit, though—an endpoint and sometimes a specific time of death.

This usually happens due to oversaturation. When a meme gets mortally flattened with overuse, it's often because celebrities and companies take notice and twist a subject to their own hollow ends. It's different from how we, the general public, overdo it, which is usually by absurd excesses, like photoshopping U.S. Senator Bernie Sanders out of the viral photo that captured him in a lawn chair with mittens on during the 2021 presidential inauguration and placing him in the UFC's Octagon, performing an armbar submission on a suffering opponent. Soulless corporate goliath, Amazon, would subsequently use that same viral photo of the noted socialist senator to promote their Amazon Pay product: "It's that easy. Thanks #BernieSandersMittens" their tweet read.

A daft corporate interpretation of something momentarily popular for momentary gains that usually ends in public backlash: this kind of appropriation is the final blow that takes the last gasps of the fun and meaning from a meme. That's how this system of virality works, a lifecycle as predictable as our own. There's almost a gamesmanship to it. Every online entity competes to see how many times it can bludgeon a subject before it's dust. Then when the feeder winds up empty and broken on the ground, we wait for someone to hang it back up anew.

AMAZING FACTS ABOUT CAMELS

T<small>HEIR</small> <small>GOAL WAS VAST</small> but simply stated:

"*Pooptime* aims to redefine entertainment and breaking news for our social generation."

A big goal. I imagine others looking at this ad on the ZipRecruiter job board might've been intimidated by the scope of *Pooptime*'s objective. Not me.

"Whether by simply putting a smile on someone's face with a funny video or by engaging our audience in social issues important to them, we strive to make a positive difference."

Pooptime is determined to make a *difference*. So how do they do that?

"We are at the forefront of reporting on the world's latest news, telling authentic shareable stories in real-time, with our original features documenting uniqueness in culture and society."

That'll do it. *Pooptime* is a website looking for *content creators*. The all-encompassing term that has swallowed writers, photographers, videographers, visual artists, musicians, scientists, bakers, broadcasters, bicycle mechanics, arborists—the list does not end.

It can't, because content can always be created and applied, even if it's just a list of the people making it—a content ouroboros.

I was looking for a job. No, I was in desperate need of a job, so my resume took on some quick and sudden changes in language: like a diner menu with items covered in painter's tape, bunched Sharpie'd-on letters spelling out the new, improved, dear-God-I-hope-people-like-this-one dishes.

"Writer" had been phased out. I was now, coincidentally, a "content creator." I went to *Pooptime*'s website to research the kinds of difference-making content they were creating and was immediately taken by a selection of article headlines.

RIP to the Celebrities that Sadly Passed Away in 2018 (Rest in Peace!)

5 Embarrassing Sports Moments That Made Them Say FML!

Beware of Butt Lifts: Someone Just DIED from Getting One

Amazing Facts About Camels – The King of The Desert

There was a lot to unpack there. I wanted to chide the authors for their RIP redundancy; however, scolding someone for offering too many condolences seems petty. Glamour shots of Vern Troyer, Mac Miller, and Aretha Franklin sit awkwardly above the headline. The article lede explains its purpose:

"2018 has been a sad year with lots of shocking and unexpected deaths of well-known and well-loved celebrities. Here are a few we (*Pooptime*) would like to commemorate the lives of."

I imagined how *Pooptime* would commemorate my death: "Another Young Life Flushed Away Too Soon." People on toilets around the world reading my tribute content, tears streaming down their straining faces before they click on the best, most embarrassing FML sports moments—an antidote to the sadness they're enduring.

Maybe that was how Pooptime was "making a difference?" Most outlets have no hesitation when it comes to delivering important, devastating news, but rarely do they offer an immediate upper: a stupid-funny or feel-good story that serves to balance one's emotions. The deluge of *New York Times* push notifications that storm my phone with details on soul-crushing policy changes, sensationalized political theatre, and the play-by-play of fascism's rise around the world, is taxing. They add weight to a sack of hopelessness that hangs off the front of my brain, slowly filling each day with each story until my head hangs so low that I am unable to look anyone in the eye; all I can see are my shoes and the steadily crumbling ground they're walking on.

But, after reading those stories, I moved on to the next suggested article, which included a video of former NBA player Joakim Noah hilariously blowing a free-throw shot, the ball floating listlessly out of his hands and travelling a mere three feet in the air before bouncing unceremoniously towards the sideline; and now I might guffaw and slap my forehead in a total FML moment that puts a hole in the sadness-bladder, draining it and allowing me to lift my head back up to the world around me.

That was work I could see myself doing. I wanted to help people. I wanted to make a difference. Even if it's small things, like lifting moods or warning people about butt lifts—*they might KILL you!* I could be giving people more time on this planet through *Pooptime*. I mean, the ideas I have for positive, life-affirming content are endless: a photo essay featuring cats posing with works of classic Russian literature, the photos bearing captions like "The Kitties Karamazov," "Crime and Purr-nishment," "Cats and Kittens," "The Death of Fluffy Tummy and Other Stories"; an expose on the best sandwiches I've ever had; or a list of celebrities who I always confuse with other celebrities, along with a few paragraphs and maybe an infographic that explores the origins of that confusion and gives a concrete solution—*in conclusion, Constance Zimmer is not Natasha Leggero.*

The job posting asks you to submit some samples of your own content to see if it fits what *Pooptime* is trying to achieve. I read a few more of their articles to better understand the *Pooptime* "voice" and "vision." While scrolling through the website, one word kept pestering me like a fly, landing on the back of my mind and digging an obvious proboscis into whatever area my common sense had been sleeping in up until that point. That question was, *why?* Why are you looking at this? Why did you click on that job posting? Are you *this* desperate? Everything on the site is crass, exploitative, and, as their names suggests—shit. The butt lift article ends with this:

"The clinic is waiting for the results of [the] post-mortem before making any further statements. We are sad to hear about the tragic results of this procedure and wish the best to [the deceased's] family. The moral of the story? Beware of butt lifts!"

The disconnection between sincerity and "content" is a vacuum where compassion is warped as it becomes weaponized for clicks. *Pooptime* listed the deceased's actual name in their spammy, soulless article. Who are these pieces for? Does anyone enjoy this? Why would you name your website *Pooptime*? Like the job posting, their contributor's page tells me to submit my content for review. I read on and learn that if your work is accepted, compensation comes in the form of the exposure of having your writing featured on *Pooptime*—you don't even get paid for shitting into the void. Which, in retrospect, is obvious. No one gets paid for articles with titles like, "This Dog Selfie is The Best Thing Ever." The site was all a ruse to exploit writers looking for experience. But I knew that. I still clicked through. *Why?* I don't think I ever seriously considered dumping a load of content for them, but some sliver of hope was there. A prick under the arm that guided my mouse to their webpage, along with the thought that it was possible to get paid *to write*.

There are innumerable sites like this all over the internet. Dark, hapless digital sphincters that squeeze off nugs of "content" without purpose or direction besides mindless monetary gain. Because for every turd someone clicks on, the site gets a tiny slice of Google Ad revenue. In other words, it's a front, a scheme, a scam—a defining trait of the Internet age. The sack of hopelessness sunk my chin to my chest. I closed all of the *Pooptime* tabs in my browser, leaving just one open:

Amazing Facts About Camels – The King of The Desert

The article was, without shame, a copy and paste of the "camel" Wikipedia page. I lifted my head to read it. What a strange, beautiful creature. Adapting to desert climate, it evolved and changed its physiology over time to ensure it would survive. Excel. Making the most of an untenable new world.

A BRIEF HISTORY

OF PEOPLE FINDING

WEIRD SHIT IN THEIR EARS

SOUND HAS AN UNCANNY way of entering the subconscious as we sleep, to execute flawless non-sequiturs in real dream-time. As I often do, I was dreaming about skateboarding. Over twenty-years on a board has led skateboarding to permeate most areas of my life. Here I was falling. Bailing. Eating shit but having a great time. My body was a fluid thing as it wrapped itself around the hand railings I was attempting and failing to grind. I could jump down twenty stairs, ragdoll to the concrete below, explode in a mess of plasma, and T-1000 myself back into form.

After an especially gruesome reconstruction, I heard scratching, like a dog at the door. Slow at first, then frantic. It was coming from my skateboard, claw marks etching themselves into the board's maple belly as it wobbled supine on the ground, the jagged grooves getting louder, deeper, until I could feel them—I shot out of bed and back into consciousness. Something was scratching at me.

I was trying to put out a fire in my brain, slapping at my head as I ran to the bathroom. Whatever it was, it was on me, in me. I used Q-tips, flushed my ear out with the tub tap. The immediate hysteria I'd woken up into made every attempt to deal with whatever was happening into a do-or-die moment. When I finally relaxed and confirmed as best as I could that whatever had been doing the scratching was either gone or hopefully never there, I went back to sleep. The bedside clock beaming a green 5 AM.

At 7:30 AM, my alarm went off. I lifted my head from the pillow and watched it fall, its silver, spindly body shooting out my ear like it had reached the end of a waterslide. I backhanded the silverfish from my bed onto the floor, the both of us still for a moment—shocked, trying to make sense of what was happening to us. I grabbed Patricia Lockwood's *Priestdaddy* from my nightstand and bludgeoned the insect, which exploded into a powdery smear across a glowing blurb from the *Boston Globe*.

This living creature had been in my head for at least two-and-a-half hours. I felt dizzy. It could have done any manner of evil things in there in that time. Laid eggs, pissed its name into a drift of earwax, penned a fascist manifesto at sextuple speed using all of its limbs.

I went under the tub tap again. Scraped out my ear canal with cotton swabs until it hurt—inspecting each end for whatever a silverfish egg might look like. "I've heard of it happening but never seen it myself," the doctor at a walk-in clinic would tell me later that day after confirming that I was not harbouring any orphan larvae. Then he told me to put diluted oil of oregano into my ear next time to flush it out—*next time?*

Concerned, I Googled the regularity of people finding bugs in their ears. In my near-panic state, I found a *SELF Magazine* article that quoted Benjamin McGrew, M.D., an associate professor in the University of Alabama at Birmingham's Department of Otolaryngology, who stated that "We see this about four to five times a year in our clinic." Which was not what I needed to read at that moment. The rest of the search results were a horror show. Listicle after listicle detailed inch-long cockroaches, centipedes, June bugs, and other skittering critters setting up camp in unsuspecting folk's orifices.

In 2012, a 92-year-old woman living with severe Alzheimer's in a nursing home was found to have fifty-seven maggots writhing inside of her, an enlarged ear canal from a surgery performed decades earlier providing a cozy home.

"It's a picture I will never, ever get out of my mind—ever," her daughter told the local CBS Chicago affiliate, recalling "hearing her scream as they were taking the maggots out of her ear."

As I continued searching, coming across videos and jpegs I struggled to look at without recoiling, I began to notice that most of these experiences, of people's ears becoming unsought havens for leggy little beings, were so heinous they seemed like works of fantasy. Surreal. Nightmarish. Most happening while in a dream state. A local Denver television station, KUSA-TV, regaled its audience with a ghoulish story of 12-year-old Wade Sholte from Parker, Colorado, who had a moth crawl into his ear as he slept. He and his family were unable to get it out.

"I was in pain. It was hurting so much," the boy said. "Every time it moved, it hit my eardrum."

They took him to the emergency room where doctors removed it with tweezers, alive. It proceeded to escape "and started flying around" the room, thumping its furry little wings in protest.

None of my findings assuaged the worries of my ear becoming a timeshare for other insects. A few of the stories seemed like ledes to the creepiest of Aesop's Fables: The parents of a sixteen-month-old in China finding a dandelion had taken root in their child's ear. Fully grown, it filled her ear canal and had to be surgically removed—a lesson in there somewhere, probably about climate change.

For years, a young boy in London, England claimed that the Tooth Fairy had jammed a baby tooth he'd lost into his ear. His parents even took him to specialists, but no one believed him. Eventually, after being diagnosed with "mucopurulent rhinorrhea," a condition in which a thick, unrelenting mucus oozes from the nose, doctors took a CT scan and inadvertently found it—the tooth.

Then there was the diamond. A photo I'd traced to an outdated medical journal showed the sparkling cut stone the size of a pinky fingernail lodged deep in someone's ear. There was no explanation of how it got there, leaving me to assume the gaps in context:

Cat burglar's attempt to stash diamond thievery?

Quirky marriage proposal gone wrong?

Inadvisable adornment of the canal?

It was strange to see something generally understood as a symbol of beauty and status shoved into a dank, fleshy hole. This was likely not its planned destination, but it was there for a purpose, however ill-judged at that moment. It made me think about the other ear intruders and what led them to fly, crawl, and grow where they did.

All of the listicles I'd frightened myself with painted these things as enemies, assailants, and aberrations of the safe human norm. But the dandelion seed was just acting by design, sprouting wherever it could. The fly that landed in the woman's ear was just looking for a safe, dark place to lay its eggs—as was the silverfish that wormed its way into mine.

Further research revealed that the silverfish was likely in the finale of an intricate, three-act mating ritual. It begins with teasing foreplay: the tiny lovers stand bug-face to bug-face, antennae quivering and rubbing against one another before they slowly retreat and return to touch antennae once more. The female then chases the male around whatever sink or attic they may occupy, in a heated game of cat and mouse. All of this before they return to face one another, taking in their partner's visage, breathing in their essence—a show of true romantic appreciation. He'll then vibrate against her and lay a sperm capsule that she brings inside of herself to fertilize her eggs. Beautiful. Gross. I doubt my ear was her number one choice; but in retrospect, it's flattering that after all of that ceremony, she would choose me as their nursery.

For days afterwards, the silverfish crashed my dreams. I'd wake up in a familiar state of shock, brushing at my head, trying to expel whatever ghosts might be crawling inside of me. But once I'd read up on them, got a better understanding of the shimmering insects, and put down some cedar shavings as a repellent, those dreams eventually stopped.

When I see silverfish now, in my bathtub or darting across the floor, I still turn them to dust—a thumb and forefinger covered with Kleenex popping them out of existence. However, I realize now that it's not their fault. Yes, it's poor decision-making on their part to be seen, to be near me, to burrow into my ear—but I know it's not malicious. I was act four in their three-act play—cut, an afterthought. I was just in their way.

TROLLING IN THE NAME OF ART

IN DESCRIBING THE BACHELOR suite sublet, I am fair. The apartment has high ceilings, a balcony, claw foot bathtub, and it's just blocks away from the Commercial Drive SkyTrain station—central to all amenities. But I level with the reader that it does get loud: with traffic's constant screech of acceleration and deceleration and the hollering of folks moving up and down Broadway, always with something unintelligible to yell into the busy night air. It can be a lot. Even with the balcony door closed, the sound will still seep in, muffled, like riding the bus with headphones on. You'll still catch snippets of strangers' conversations between whatever your music streaming service is feeding you.

That's what I say in my Craigslist "Apts/Housing" for rent post. I want the ad to include the flaws of the suite in order to be forthcoming and genuine, so that when someone reads it they don't feel like they're being put on—right up until the moment when I want them to, which happens when I mention offhand-edly that, yeah, occasionally the floor does become lava. That's when sincerity meets the absurd and the already tenuous belief one has in the validity of an anonymous online posting is tested. Was that a typo? Does the place have lava rock tile? Some readers will immediately close the tab, having no time for my bullshit, but others continue, eventually running into this:

"The apartment comes fully furnished and I've set the furniture up in such a way that when the floor does become lava, you can easily jump from couch to coffee table to office chair, etc. to reach all areas of the apartment without being reduced to ash."

Then it's clear that the post is fiction. Or it should be clear. At least that's how I designed it to be. An instance of lighthearted trolling. Instance one of fifteen. I'd scattered fourteen more of these throughout Vancouver's Craigslist page, in all categories, in the name of art. The premise was simple enough: write fictionalized Craigslist ads, have local artists create visual pieces inspired by these fake ads and exhibit their work in a gallery space alongside a screen that displays the actual anonymous responses those ads elicited from people on the world's most popular classifieds website.

But beyond watching confused dogs serpentine across parks, anticipating balls I pretended to throw (that would never land), I had no real experience with trolling. Especially online and with humans. Because humans are unpredictable, complex creatures. And when given the safety of anonymity that Craigslist provides, they will decry, denounce, uplift, engage, solicit, and offer a range of emotional reactions that are hard to prepare for. The bachelor suite sublet ad? It received over one hundred replies. Most in the vein of this one:

"Despite my concerns about the lava, I would like to come and view the suite for rent if it is still available."

And that's where my "lighthearted trolling" met reality. Vancouver is in the middle of an historic housing crisis. People are desperate. They'll wade through my stupidity if there's even an inkling of potential to find a reasonably affordable place to live. It only took 24 hours to amass those hundred earnest responses. Some of them even coming from the email addresses of friends. I deleted the post shortly after.

In another ad, placed in the "Barter" section, I played a man explaining how he inherited a beautiful mahogany dining table from his mother. I detailed a strange, sad upbringing in which all this guy had ever wanted since childhood was a dog, so now he's looking to trade this table for a pooch. It's an odd post that asks a lot of the reader. Would they even believe it? Will they feel compassion for the man? Can someone actually trade a dog for a table? There was only one response to this post. Someone with a kind heart, gently, courteously, let this fabricated man know that he can just go to the "Pet" section of Craigslist, "lots of free ones [there] ... you can probably keep your table :)"

That someone took the time to respond and help is heartening. The ability to shield one's identity on the internet usually leads to cruelty and lasciviousness, not kindness. But not to worry, the worst of humanity is still there. In a story posted in the "Missed Connections" category, I concocted a particularly stupid one-night stand, which like most quality MCs, makes multiple references to *The Exorcist* and my potential possession by a demon. The only thing that genders the author is that it's posted in "F4M." And despite the ad detailing a specific person and experience, I received nearly sixty responses. Some claimed to be the imaginary man in the story, others acknowledged it wasn't them but decided to proposition me for sex anyways. And the dick pics—I received an absolute deluge of unsolicited cocks.

The first response was a picture of an erect penis hanging clinically out of a pair of boxer briefs with the terse command: "Come downtown now. West Georgia. I can host." That came two minutes after the post went live, this man and his cock.jpeg waiting to pounce. One person brazenly sent a link to his sex tape as if that would entice.

The responses to that ad opened a small window into what I'd only imagined it was like to be a woman on the internet—the original story, again, was not asking for solicitations or graphic photos from strangers in the slightest; nevertheless, they came and it was torrential. I felt queasy watching those emails populate my inbox in real-time, notifications like red, festering boils.

But that post also received this message:

"Odd I know but you may be a sex demon as odd as that sounds! Here's a wiki link to what I'm thinking: https://en.m.wikipedia. org/wiki/Succubus"

Thanks? These were the responses I was looking for. The ones where someone shared a peculiar piece of their personality that wasn't directed by their dick. This person thought that I, the wholly imagined person in the ad, could be a succubus and they wanted to give me a heads-up. That is a fascinating kind of concern.

In the "Free" section, I posted a story about a roll of photos, taken of someone on their deathbed, that were ruined by the recently-deceased's spirit being a total perv to everyone in the room—the camera being the only thing able to capture the ghost's deviancy.

"Yes please please I want these ... I'm sorry the old guy acted so silly on a serious day and ruined your last photos of him with family but I would love to see/have these!"

Here was an anonymous person interested in the niche photographic realm of degenerate phantoms. And let's not forget the religious scholars toiling away on the site, fact-checking in the name of the heavenly father:

"To be Baptized is a sigh [sic] to the world that you have accepted Christ to be your Lord and Savour [sic]. How than [sic] do you expect to be Baptized then if you do not believe this. I am Christian and have been Baptized. Read John 3:16 God Bless."

Savour the saviour. A planted story about a practical non-believer trying to cover all of their bases by getting baptized just in case the afterlife turned out to be a real destination is what prompted that scolding and faith-based chest-thumping.

* * *

The art exhibition was about embracing a certain, known-yet-unknown darkness that comes with using the internet, like eating an apple with visible rot. Not all of the apple is brown and folding in on itself with decay or is being tunnelled through by worms, but the parts that are? They can still make you sick. And I could feel it in my gut.

It was a combination of things. I regretted trolling people looking for homes, but also learned about the level of desperation affecting people in Vancouver, which was eye-opening and painful. I thought I already knew how terrible it was to exist on the internet as a woman; but having that amount of unsolicited hard (ugh) evidence was unsettling. Our sense of reality is more flexible and, for the most part, devoid of accountability in the anonymous online space. Yet, we remain. Because, ultimately, we're creatures that thrive on connection, and we can live with the bullshit if it means getting the right kind of stranger's attention:

"I just want to say thank you for posting this add [sic] in the way you did. Def put a smile on many people's faces when looking for an apartment can be stressful."

I'm grateful if that fake ad was a relief for one person. And despite all the personal turmoil I whipped into form through some stilted effort at art, I'm grateful for Craigslist. It's not all terrible. Even under pseudonyms, some people still care. It has allowed them to express themselves, to build a community, which is the site's goal. To be a space for people selling dumbbells, stereos, and swords. A forum to talk about politics, gaming, and the cosmos. A place to find a job, an apartment, and even love.

THE LAST WHOLESOME CORNER
OF THE INTERNET

MOST ACCIDENTS ON THE internet are not pleasant: a slip of the mouse shooting off an embarrassing typo-laden message to a potential employer before you're able to take care of the squiggly red lines; private private photos mistakenly getting tweeted out onto a public profile instead of in the DMs; an attempt to illegally download an episode of *True Detective* foiled by a torrent carrying ransomware—Mahershala Ali somewhere in the Ozarks shaking his head disapprovingly.

But sometimes—just sometimes—you can stumble, trip, and fall into purity. A single skipped letter in a word brings you to a true, untainted piece of the web. This happened to a coworker who attempted to reach his Gmail account but forgot a crucial consonant. Amused, he shared his finding in an office Slack thread: gail.com.

This domain, an unflashy FAQ page belonging to the eponymous Gail, says it received almost *two-million* visits in 2015—83% of those from unique IP addresses.

"Q: Why is your website so popular? Are you one of those famous people that no one knows why they're famous?

A: No, I'm not famous. It seems likely that most visitors simply mistype gmail.com and end up visiting gail.com by mistake."

Where those millions of unintentional visitors are landing is, in itself, another accident. The page's nine, simple, funny Q&As act as a historical guide: Gail's husband bought her gail.com as a birthday gift in 1996, a present purchased eight years before the advent of Gmail. The domain was supposed to be a proto-blog. An online vanity plate. A bobblehead made in your lover's likeness. They had no idea what was to come.

1996 was a starkly different time for the internet. It was a hominid evolving at dial-up speed—'96 the birth year of *Ask Jeeves*. Then things started to pick up. Fast. The number of global internet users nearly doubled between 1996 and 1997. An explosion of people all sharing, searching, and looking to create their own online homes.

"Q: Interested in selling gail.com?

A: Sorry, no."

Gail started to get offers from people wanting to buy her OG domain: other Gails with designs to be *the* Gail in the new digital realm. Each time, she declined. Then in 2006, the cordiality of those offers expired. A ceramic tile manufacturing company out of Brazil, also called Gail, tried to take the domain name from her. The company argued in a World Intellectual Property Organization (WIPO) complaint that it had trademarked "Gail" in several Latin American countries, which gave it legal dominion over the name. *Her name.* They accused Gail and her husband of having no "legitimate interest" in the domain, and of registering it in "bad faith" —nearly a decade previous—with the intent of "abusive practice[s]."

Gail and her husband countered the company's points, saying the complaint was an attempt at "Reverse domain hijacking." WIPO agreed, stating that one cannot claim copyright over a common word or name, swiftly rejecting Brazilian Gail's complaint.

"Q: Are you interested in monetizing gail.com?

A: No, but thanks for asking."

If you squint, Gail could be seen as squatting on her domain. The site does figure to be lucrative, given the hits it receives; but she refuses to squeeze any bucks out of it with Google Ads or anything of the sort. She is not a scammer cybersquatting on prince.com. A link to the digital rights group, the Electronic Frontier Foundation is her only "ad."

Reading her FAQ, and seeing the morals and levity that have guided Gail through the strange evolution of her website—from an online family photo album to an artifact memorializing victory over corporate marauders—together create a much-needed reprieve from the noxious morass that much of the internet has become. Is Gail's page a statement? A finger in the eye of a stilted, capitalist system? Or is she someone simply wanting to exist freely on the web?

Gail didn't respond to my request for an interview, so I don't know. Neither has Kevin, her husband and respondent in the WIPO case. A WHOIS search reveals that he not only registered gail.com in 1996, but also kevin.org—another simple, straightforward page laid out in a style similar to his wife's.

Kevin's site details a career spanning from Google to NASA to SpaceX. It's a breakdown of a man who has made technology his life. Gail's gift is one that makes perfect sense.

These domains were supposed to be matching His & Hers aprons. Identical, designated La-Z-Boys stationed in front of the television. Twin faded dolphin tattoos etched into upper biceps while in Miami on a whimsical first romantic getaway—reminders of place, time, and person.

"Q: Why isn't there any content here? Can't you at least throw up a picture of your cat for the Internet to check out?

A: Sorry, I have a cat, but she's pretty unexciting by internet standards."

Whatever Gail's reasons may be, they've had an effect. A search of "gail.com" on Twitter shows multiple instances a day of people following their typos to her site and sharing how they've been charmed by its wholesomeness and buoyed by its ethics. It's become a small light shimmering in the darkness of our timelines. Her page a pixelated diamond in the digital rough.

SEND FLOWERS

THERE IS A "SEND FLOWERS" button on the Mission View Funeral Chapel website's homepage. If you click on it, you are given the option to have flowers delivered from a local florist in Lac La Biche to an upcoming Mission View funeral service of your choice. All you have to do is pick out which flowers you want, confirm your order, and press *send*.

Every few months, I ask Google to take me to missionview.ca. This is how I stay up to date with my hometown—an admittedly morbid check-in. I haven't lived in the LLB for nearly two decades, but I still recognize the people whose obituaries populate the website. The Cadieuxs, Cardinals, Lewiskis, Desjarlais, Wowks, Waines, Bouviers, Bouchards—names from my childhood that were constants. Teachers, shopkeeps, clergy. These were the adults my preteen self would look up at as I trekked from V&H Drive-In to Fiddler's Food & Gas—one end of Main Street to the other.

The eponymous Art of Art's Music, where I got my first guitar. Dead. The patriarch and owner of a local contracting empire, whose heavy machinery is ubiquitous at construction sites around town and leases up in the oil patch. Dead. The kind woman with the concentrated plumes of white hair who used to smile at me from her pew when I'd look around the church restlessly during Sunday Mass, my head lolling backwards while I counted the treated beams crossing the convex ceiling like ribs. Dead.

Those are the expected deaths. The passing of people who've experienced the lion's share of what the general human existence has to offer, who have survived different eras, economies, Prime Ministers, technologies, and are now just naturally calling it a life.

But each time I visit missionview.ca, an obituary or two always gives me pause. It'll take me a moment as the connections are made, memories dusted off at the back of my brain and put back into place to make sense of who I'm seeing. A friend from elementary school who dared me to join him in dripping hot glue onto our hands—a test of courage and strength that would determine our burgeoning manhood. Dead.

My first crush from a grade above. After school, as we'd all wait for the bus, she'd inexplicably come and talk to me, ask how my day was, tease me about my skateboard, and tell me about her and her sister's latest aerial achievements on their family's trampoline. Dead. The only person I'd ever been in a physical fight with, the both of us rolling around on the linoleum of our middle school hallway until I ended up on top and started thumping him on the forehead with my purple full-arm cast; and afterwards, as we waited outside of the principal's office for our punishment, I fished around in the pockets of my giant, billowing late-90s jeans. There was a can of Coke in each one; they'd been there during our skirmish, safely swimming around in my knockoff SAAN Store JNCOs. Coyly, I offered him one, expecting it to explode upon opening, an exclamation point on what I had already perceived as a victory. He declined. Dead.

My Grandmother often plays spoiler to my missionview.ca check-ins. On the phone, after I update her on my life (what I'm working on, what an Instagram is) and dodge her question about when I am going to get married and give her a great-grandchild, she tells me about her life. In the old folks' home, death is the news. I get the inside scoop on who has moved on to that spacious one-bedroom unit with a mini fridge in the sky. Her updates make sense, as dark as they are. In seniors' housing, your community is made up almost entirely of housemates competing with you in a more sedentary version of a *Survivor* immunity challenge. Specifically, the one where contestants see who can stand on the top of a wooden pole the longest without falling into the water. *Sploosh*. Swallowed by time. Who you are, were, and ever would be, gone with a splash. The only public evidence you were ever on a pole with the rest is the pixelated photo accompanying your obit on missionview.ca.

A slider bar on the homepage lets you swipe through the recently deceased like a macabre Tinder. During this visit, I'm here to send flowers. I swipe on my great Aunt Jean. Her page consists of an obit tab listing the familial connections, the pallbearers. There's a tab for details on the service: Date, time, location. It'll be at the St. Catherine's Catholic Church with its treated wood ribs spanning its high, heavenly torso.

Under the "Send Flowers" tab are sixty-seven different arrange-ments and even a fruit basket to choose from. There's the "Simply Stated Casket Spray," a tasteful spread of red roses to plop on top of the body. The "Unending Circle in Pale Shades of Colour" is a wreath of carnations, mums, and waxflowers ringing a photo of your loved one. There are three versions of the "Unending Circle in Pale Shades of Colour" to choose from: Good, Better, and Best.

They range in price from $149.99 - $249.99. How much do you love the dead? Good enough? Better than good enough? Best of all? They've got you covered.

A small porcelain Jesus sits in the centre of the "Garden of Serenity Bouquet." White roses, snapdragons, and lilies sprouting around him. The "radiant flowers will be a source of comfort to loved ones during a time of loss. Your thoughtfulness will be remembered," the website states.

My thoughtfulness will be remembered? Will anyone remember if I'm not "thoughtful?" If I don't hover over the "Best" button, press down, and drop a couple hundred? What if I pick "Designer's Choice" for a measly $79.99? The cover image for that option is just a big, burgundy question mark, its dot a carnation. I scroll back up to the top: "Allow us to take care of your expression of sympathy," the header implores.

There's one more tab on Aunt Jean's page: "Tribute Wall." On it are comments from friends, family and even folks representing local businesses. The messages are kind. Recalling memories. Uplifting her and her loved ones. Thoughts, prayers. There's an option, along with leaving a note, to "Light a Candle." This leaves a small digital graphic of a lit candle, some with doves or roses on them, flickering beside your tribute. If you want, you can embed a YouTube video, which, thankfully, no one has done. The digitization of mourning is a clumsy thing. Also on the tribute page is a history of those who have "sent."

"UNENDING CIRCLE IN PALE SHADES OF COLOUR was sent by [a family friend]."

"A CLASSIC FRUIT BASKET was sent by [a former colleague]."

I decide against flowers and light a candle. Its cartoonish flame is steady, ignited by a click of the mouse. That's the type of thoughtfulness that gets remembered in this age. Affordable. Effective. Timestamped, even. A fruit basket's cantaloupe and honeydew will be forgotten. Digested. Excreted. Each time I come back here to see who has fallen off the pole, this candle will be here, burning.

MY PERSONAL MEDIUM, BRIAN ENO

AT A DINNER PARTY a friend pulled out her phone.

"I have a meme you need to see."

It's a photo of a contemplative chihuahua in a bubble bath, the pink shower cap on its head glowing from the candles placed around the tub. Above the dog, black text on white background reads,

"Capricorn after their discrete approach to love costs them the person of their life because they took too long to open up and refused to express any feelings until things felt secure, which would've taken up to 360 business days."

It's funny. It's accurate. I tell my friend I feel like I'm being attacked.

Astrology is something that has fascinated me from a distance. Listening to friends talk about which planets belong to which signs, who's compatible with whom, having people read my birth chart with various reactions of delight and horror—it's fun. And increasingly popular. Astrology memes are a fixture on social media. There are hundreds of astrology apps you can add your friends to, to collect and compare their charts like they're relational

Pokémon cards. Deeper in the commercial realm, you'll find Etsy has an entire astrology marketplace. From a "You Are My Favourite Libra" candle set, to constellation mousepads, to a T-shirt with Garfield standing smug, arms crossed under a squiggly font:

"Aquarians are normal. The rest of the world is weird." (A quick Google search reveals that Garfield is actually a Gemini.)

Even YouPorn has released sex horoscopes. "Easily bored, you absolutely hate routine in the bedroom," Garfield's Gemini profile says, which seems fitting. Articles in the *The Atlantic* and *The New Statesman* by Julie Beck and Amelia Tate, respectively, attribute this boom to the current social climate.

"There is some evidence that in times of turmoil—both political and economic—people are drawn to paranormal beliefs," a behavioural scientist in the *New Statesman* piece explains. "There is much more insecurity about jobs for the current generation of young people than in the past, and for liberal millennials in particular, the world has suddenly gone a little crazy ... Considerable research on astrology suggests that believers are drawn to it for a sense of control."

That same article quotes Motherpeace Tarot, a deck company that's been around since the '70s, as having seen a "268 percent increase in sales in the past six months." If you wanted to make the connection between that uptick and the swirling toilet bowl of politics and culture that was 2018, it would make sense.

The Atlantic's piece, besides having this stunner of a boomer pull quote: "The kids these days and their memes ... ," continues the idea that astrology serves as a comfort to its followers, whether or not they really believe in it. It's a "relief, in a time of division, not to have to choose. It can be freeing, in a time that values black and white, ones and zeros, to look for answers in the gray."

That makes sense to me because I do pretty much the same thing—looking to an outside power for guidance and support. But I believe 100 percent. Not in astrology, tarot, or any of history's many deities, mind you. I believe in Brian Eno.

* * *

I stared at the computer screen as I finished towelling off my hair. Staring back at me was a story I'd been stuck working on for the past three days. The narrative wouldn't budge. I deleted paragraphs, shuffled them around, and pasted them back into place. Once I'd exhausted ways to rearrange the words, I decided to consult my Oblique Strategies card set. Its Wikipedia page describes Oblique Strategies as "A card-based method for promoting creativity ... each card offers a challenging constraint intended to help artists break creative blocks by encouraging lateral thinking." Created by Brian Eno and Peter Schmidt to help them out of creative slumps in the studio, the cards, I find, are also a helpful exercise for general living. Usually. That morning I pulled a card that just said, "water." It was almost comical in its unhelpfulness.

I backspaced and Command+C'd a few more times before giving up and going to the sink, holding a cup under the faucet for an inordinate amount of time before realizing that nothing was coming out of it. I went to the bathroom sink. Nothing. I tried the shower I'd just used. Only the tired screech of pipes pushing out air.

There hadn't been any signs put up around the building warning about a water shutoff, something the building manager usually did. I called her and was told there'd been an emergency, which had happened not even an hour ago. *Water*. Had the Oblique Strategy card predicted this? It was strangely prescient. I considered it a coincidence until I pulled another card a few days later. "Tidy up." It felt like an explicit directive. Given the chance weirdness of a few days previous, I played along, cleaning my apartment from top to bottom.

Even if nothing came of it, hey, at least my place would look nice. Perhaps I'd duped myself into responsibility. Two hours after the last Swiffer WetJet streaks had dried, I got a text from my stepmother. She and my grandmother had flown into town unannounced for a quick visit and wanted to see if I was free for dinner. "We can meet you at yours." I looked at the gleaming laminate flooring, the clean laundry neatly hung in the closet, and the sleek black Oblique Strategies case on the shelf.

"Thanks, Brian," I whispered to the room.

"Is there something missing?" a card asked one morning. I looked around and patted my body and pants pockets. Lifted the couch cushions and pushed aside the canned lentils in the cupboard. Searching for something that is missing when you don't know what that missing thing is, is not an easy task. I went through my calendar and Facebook notifications—no birthday well-wishings had gone unwished, no errands un-run. I sifted through my emails, checking to see if I'd forgotten to respond to anything pressing.

In the spam folder—a heinous vacuum of all-caps boner pill offers and personal messages from the directors of Citibank and the International Monetary Fund politely letting me know of the million-dollar bank transfers that awaited me if I'd just take a second to follow a link and provide some personal information—was an email that didn't belong. An actually urgent message from the Canada Council for the Arts that had, for whatever reason, wound up among the turgid, sweaty-palmed, grammatically flawed emails of the spam folder. I had forgotten to attach an important document to a grant application, and if I didn't submit it by end of day, I'd be ineligible for funding. If it weren't for the Oblique Strategies card worrying me into scouring the corners of my inbox, I would've missed the deadline.

Brian Eno was acting as my personal medium; that much was clear. I decided to push aside my reservations, place my skepticism neatly in the bedside table drawer, and become a full-on, unabashed, fundamental Oblique Strategist. I now pull a card each morning for guidance and turn to Brian before any decision of consequence, or one that might stir any nerves.

"Hey Brian, I've got a job interview coming up and don't feel confident that my resume is strong enough. What should I do?"

Try faking it!

"Hi Brian, it's been a stressful week and I haven't been able to decompress. Any suggestions?"

Do nothing for as long as possible.

"It's me again, Brian. I've got a blistering hot take that I want to tweet, but I'm a little worried that I don't fully understand the subject at hand and might come off as an idiot. Whaddyah think?

Question the heroic approach.

So far, the cards haven't steered me wrong. Whatever power they hold for me can likely be attributed to the "comfort" and "control" that behavioural scientists claim is the appeal of tarot, religion, and faith-based practices in general. But why *these* cards? Why Eno? With Oblique Strategies, there's no cultural baggage and demanded fealty of religion or the complicated cross-narratives of astrology. It's a simple, straightforward clairvoyance.

When deciding whether to write this piece, I consulted the cards:

Towards the insignificant.

THINGS YOU CAN NOW SHOOT LASERS AT

I WISH I COULD'VE LAUGHED when my dad told me that doctors would stick a laser inside his body to blast apart his enlarged prostate like it was a game of fleshy Space Invaders. It would've been nice to double over and howl incredulously when he clarified that they wouldn't stick the laser up his butt, as I'd originally assumed, but shoot it straight into his penis. "Laser dick" is just objectively funny. But I can't laugh because I'm worried. He can't pee. A catheter, taped to his leg and attached to a bag concealed in his work slacks, slowly fills with tired spurts of urine throughout the day. He's 54. Too young for that. "It's massive," the doctor told my dad about his prostate while maneuvering a slender camera up his rectum, immediately knowing surgery was needed, peering at the engorged gland like a mystical orb; the answers right there, projected on its surface.

While I look up the laser-blast technique, I put my dad on speaker, reciting to him what the Mayo Clinic website tells me: "During prostate laser surgery, your doctor inserts a scope through the tip of your penis into the tube that carries urine from your bladder (urethra). The prostate surrounds the urethra. A laser passed through the scope delivers energy that shrinks or removes excess tissue that is preventing urine flow."

That's much more palatable phrasing for what a laser does—*delivers energy*. It's like a mediocre review of an off-off-Broadway play. I had no idea lasers could be used like that. What immediately comes to mind whenever the subject of lasers arises are Stormtroopers. The puzzlingly fearsome, bumbling, schlub-shooters whose blaster-fire is so inaccurate that it's inspired a whole sub-genre of YouTube video compilations mocking the incompetent foot soldiers for consistently and historically missing their targets. As my dad details his visit to the doctor, I picture a Stormtrooper, clad in shiny molded body armour, trying to line up a shot right down his urethra. It's not comforting.

I try to sub the Stormtrooper out for Luke in an X-Wing, hovering above the table in the operating room, waiting for the nurse's signal before firing off a couple of casual, obviously on the mark, laser blasts that shimmer down the impossibly narrow corridor to hit their target first try, no problem. Prostate vaporized—a new hope realized. The Rebels, in scrubs, rejoice.

✳ ✳ ✳

Lasers aren't just for destroying intergalactic super weapons and carving prostates back to normal size. They also whiten teeth. My dentist told me about the procedure after I lamented the coffee stain annexing more and more territory on my right canine. He mimed spreading the special peroxide gel over my teeth as though they were Chicklet-sized pieces of toast, explaining how he would then use a powerful hand-held laser to "excite" the gel, essentially bleaching my teeth. "While you would be exposed to some infrared emissions—so don't do this if you're pregnant or lactating—it's generally pretty safe."

He handed me a pamphlet about the laser whitening. I flipped through a few flimsy pages of stock-photo smiles beaming encouragingly, iridescent. On the last page was a bullet-point list of benefits.

- Dramatically whiter teeth
- It's *laser* fast
- Long-lasting effect
- The increased self-confidence that comes from a more attractive smile

Those were all things I was interested in, especially the last one. But not for the $1,000 price tag. That was a fair chunk of cash to pay to have a radiant, irradiated smile. I wondered if my dad's prostate laser-blasting would expose him to radiation because prostate cancer is a scary beast and you've got to be careful with what you get up to down there—I finally clued in. How could it have taken so long? I felt like an idiot. Why else would he need this surgery? A silence hung between us. I listened to him rinse a dish in a sink 1,200 kilometres away. That distance doubled, tripled, as I tried to figure out what to say, dancing around it.

"So ... is this ... your penis lasering ... indicative of anything else?"

* * *

I needed to relax. Days, weeks, generations fit inside the quiet between my question and his answer. I thought about dogs—that would help. Cute dogs. Happy dogs. Fluffy dogs. Lasers. Running dogs. Jumping dogs. Lasers. Petting dogs. Lasers. Laser dogs. Dog lasers. Those exist. Of course they do. There's a laser for anything and everything. What does a laser do for a dog? The question is, what can't it do?

Does your dog have muscle, ligament, or tendon injuries? Shoot a laser at the pooch. Is your furry companion suffering from back pain? *PewPewPew*. Have you noticed Rex pawing at his ear? Clear up that infection by shining a laser down your canine's ear canal like a flashlight in a storm drain you dropped your keys into. Gingivitis? Blast those gums with gamma rays. Hot spots and open wounds? You know what to do. Arthritis and hip dysplasia? Spark those joints with some hot-ass beams of light. Degenerative disc disease? Laser therapy can help.

Do dogs get acne? Because there's a laser for that, too. Imagine if teenage me had known? Instead of lancing the glowing ball of pus that stayed on the tip of my nose for the last semester of eighth grade, with a safety pin, which ultimately got it infected and left a nice divot in my flesh, I could've just shot a fucking laser at it.

Lasers don't eliminate just zits; they can also nuke fat cells. A cold laser stimulates the cells, needling them until they cannot take it and collapse, giving up their contents like they've been shaken down for lunch money. Plastic surgeons suggest that you do a 40-minute session three times a week, for two weeks, to get the desired results from the procedure. That desired result being the destruction of your cellular makeup.

But where does all of the plaque and coffee stains and gingivitis and arthritis and hip dysplasia and pimples and pain go after being zapped? And where does every trace bit of radiation released from every singular laser go after doing the zapping? Does it all just disappear? Vaporized like my dad's prostate? Can you ever make a thing gone for good? Where do I aim the laser to vaporize my fear and anxiety? Will the disparate particles of my worry ever find each other again like old friends? Old friends eager to reunite and get back to what they do best.

He tells me it isn't cancer, just a bout of benign prostatic hyperplasia—something that just *happens* to people. Then he hits one of his common refrains: "It's just one of those things, where yah have to go, *whatever*." I can hear his shoulders shrugging through the phone. That *whatever* has been prescribed for things like the whimpering Albertan economy, Justin Trudeau in general, and the continued stresses of work. Things that wear on him like an angle grinder, that he has come to accept because that's just life and sometimes all you can do is sigh when the gravity in your world gets altered and slams you into the earth, untethering you from it altogether.

That's another thing that lasers can do. *Interferometry*. The detection of shifts of gravitational waves.

WHO PISSED ON MY BALCONY

ON BOXING DAY, THE day after my girlfriend's dad's curling partner revealed that he'd contracted COVID, subsequently putting us all at risk of a festive holiday exposure, I was isolated back at home in Vancouver, alone, staring at what appeared to be a stream of frozen piss on the balcony of my third-floor, bachelor-suite apartment. Whose piss it was, I did not know. It hadn't been there before I'd taken my ritual post-lunch nap; but once up, I'd gone to the window to watch a Dark-eyed Junco pick away at the suet block feeder, and a shimmering yellow flash caught my eye.

I opened the sliding door and did what any reasonably curious person would do: I got on my hands and knees and smelt the frozen piss. Unfortunately, this didn't give me any answers; its aroma had frozen off like a frostbitten toe. My index finger edged close to the piss-flow's solid outer edge, where the yellow was darker, more potent. Would knowing the texture of this icebound mystery-discharge help identify who or what had done this? Likely not. I pulled my hand back, its flesh goose-pimpled from the cold.

Here, in my own home, where I'd been hiding my potentially COVID-ridden body from the rest of the world, a mystery was unfurling—and I now had something to do. Could it have been the birds? House sparrows, starlings, bushtits, chickadees, Dark-eyed

Juncos, and even the occasional crow will frequent my feeders, often shitting all over the place. But I hadn't known them to take leaks, especially ones of such volume. "Do birds piss big?" I asked Google. Canada's public broadcaster explained:

> "Birds and mammals produce nitrogenous waste products that must be excreted from the body. A byproduct of this waste in both, is ammonia. Mammals, including humans, convert the ammonia to urea, which is excreted in urine. Birds convert the ammonia to uric acid, which appears as the thick, white paste we commonly think of as bird poop,"

So, if it wasn't the birds, who could it be? Being on the third floor makes my balcony nearly impossible to access unless one is blessed with the gift of flight, a ladder, or dexterous little rodent claws. Perhaps a squirrel? It seemed doubtful, as I hadn't seen one on the balcony in my decade-plus years of living here, but you never know. "Do squirrels piss big?" I asked Google.

After watching a seven-minute YouTube video titled "Gray Squirrels Mark Territory With Pee," I concluded that while squirrels can piss pretty big, it wasn't big enough to match the frozen piss pond on my balcony. However, I did learn, thanks to a *Washington Post* "Answer Man" column from 2012, that "Squirrels are among species—deer are another—where the mother uses her mouth to carry her offspring's poo and pee away from the nest. This is to protect her litter from predators." Okay!

By the next day, I had reached an impasse. Who or what else could be the culprit? Should I be worried? Was there some Jack the Pisser type out there letting it leak all over town? I FaceTimed my girlfriend and held the phone centimetres from the frozen urine. "I don't know!" She shouted as I begged for an answer. I hung up and inspected the snowfall on my balcony closely. It was pocked with hard-to-decipher bird tracks. Their paths were twisting, doubling back on themselves. Indecisive. Second-guessing. The anxious ambling of the guilty. If only birds pissed big.

Then I turned to the dividing wall separating my balcony from my neighbour's. They were new, and I had yet to run into them in the hallway. All I knew was that they received as many as three packages from Amazon per day and that they loved The Tragically Hip. I'd heard them sing along to all of the album *Road Apples* and even quietly joined in during their rendition of "Twist My Arm."

That was all suspicious; but unfortunately, for my investigation, the piss fjord on my balcony was too small to be the markings of a full-bladdered Hip fan. I'd run into another wall. Was this a mystery wee I'd just have to live with? Its memory an ever-present yellow stain as its perpetrator remained on the loose, whiz instrument in hand or paw, ready, waiting to defile?

The following day I woke to a FaceTime call from my girlfriend. Her dad had tested negative, which meant we were likely also in the clear. The sun poured through the balcony window. I opened the sliding door and felt its warmth. Then I got to my knees and pressed the small button on my phone to turn its camera around.

"The piss is melting, do you see? Can you see it?" The phone centimetres from the liquid as it began to extend towards the front of the balcony, forging a new path forward.

SMOOTH BLACK MARBLE

THE BUS IS MOSTLY the same. I run to catch it like I always have. The train is as it's always been. Empty, then full in an instant. I walk into the airport like I've done many times before. Today they shoot a laser at my head to check my temperature as I walk through security. All familiar but slightly askew.

My mask muffles my voice and I accept an Americano with "Paul" scrawled across its side. Close enough. There are still in-flight movies, and I still watch the little map and our little airplane drag its way across provinces instead. The rental car accelerates, and I shift lanes and I take exits and I stop to piss in a farmer's field just as the farmer rounds the corner in a horse-drawn carriage and clomps through the ditch in my direction. Same as it ever was.

Lac La Biche, Alberta, my hometown, is so close to what I've known, but now feels a little lighter in the palm. Hamar's Grocery, where my mother used to buy cheap cigarettes from my aunt, is gone—cut out of the skyline and replaced by a parking lot and barbershop. The old V&H Drive-In Diner: erased. The building and its giant cartoon UFO mascot that hovered above were destroyed in a fire deemed "deliberately set."

The childhood home I lived in with my mother and stepfather, sold years ago, still has the same white stucco siding, but the burgundy garage door is faded, and shrubs are overgrown on the lawn. My memories of running around the yard don't quite play here anymore: bunny ears catching static. The neighbours across the street are new. Or old by now. But new to me.

People from my past are still here. A few have multiplied; others are in the tenth year of homeownership while I continue to pay a mortgage worth of rent on a Vancouver bachelor suite. Many folks are now gone. Some moved, like me; others died, like my grandfather, who passed last winter. His interment ceremony postponed until it was considered safe enough for a small number of us to gather. Now, here I am.

While time and circumstance continue at their rushed and ragged pace, I try to take note of the constants. Places and memories that persist. One in particular stands out here. The first quarter-pipe I ever dropped in on—a hollow, booming metallic structure part of a modular skatepark installed and announced as "temporary"—remains a quarter of a century later.

The hours I'd spent making noise on this thing were incalculable. The flesh peeled from my body after falling on the searing steel in peak summer heat, measurable by the splotched scars on my elbow. It was here, sending echoes across the park, that I first gave in to skateboarding, letting it become not so much a pastime as a loving, vindictive, all-consuming jinn. This new spirit demanded my constant attention, whether I was riding my board or not.

Beyond possession, skateboarding introduced me to an entirely new culture and community. In every subsequent town I'd move to with my father after leaving Lac La Biche, in every subsequnet town I'd move to with my father, this toy was an automatic icebreaker with other skateboarders. The skate videos I'd collect were a gateway to whole new realms of music and art.

These are all well-worn clichés in the life of anyone who skates: patterns of growth and discovery as determined as puberty. None are more tired than the idea that riding a skateboard reshapes how one interacts with the physical world when the angles of urban architecture curve hospitably, allowing benches and curbs and stairs and embankments to become playthings, testing grounds.

The reverie and determination required to become a committed skateboarder often reveal a new emotional world to the rider, too. Grit, courage, creativity—all gemstones unearthed if you do it for long enough. Skateboarding would also teach me how to grieve.

✳ ✳ ✳

Not far from the skatepark in Lac La Biche is William J. Cadzow Healthcare Centre. Named after the father of my older half-brother's father, it's also home to a loading dock that I used to ride my skateboard off of with the grimacing hope that it'd join me.

Eighteen or so years ago, I nollie-kickflipped from the top of the loading dock to the halting asphalt below. With no one there to witness this, my memory is the only proof of the make; trust me, if you will. The following February, my stepfather died in hospice on the other side of the building.

When my mother phoned from a province away to tell me that the cancer that softened his bones and hollowed his cheeks had finally won, the first thing I did was grab my skateboard. My living father drove me to the skatepark, and I pushed myself as hard as I could for hours until my body ached and could no longer meet the demands of my mind, which lay open and empty.

The following summer, my mother suffered a severe mental health crisis after the loss of her husband and the creeping collapse of her sign-making shop. In this hospital, she refused to see my brother or me until we "reigned ourselves in" and gave ourselves to her god. Our souls were dirtied, caked in sin we couldn't understand. It was a distressing, disorienting time for a fifteen-year-old, to be sure. In the aftermath, I would watch Ryan Gallant's section in Transworld Skateboarding's video "First Love" on repeat just to find comfort in the lyrics of the Five Stairstep's "O-o-h Child," which served as the soundtrack.

This became the way I learned how to handle hurt: by skating into and away from it, even if all I could manage was a short distance, a few hours at best—a skate video played on repeat. This, which might be categorized as a coping method, is another cliché in this world. Skateboarding, in its youth, was known for attracting misfits, outsiders, kids from broken homes and troubled backgrounds—those needing an escape.

Follow skate media for any amount of time and that storyline will still show up. It's hardcoded into our collective lore. "Skateboarding saved my life" is a mantra you'll hear any bro at the skatepark spew if they've Bogarted the joint for long enough. And to be honest, as corny as that is, I don't know where I'd be without skateboarding either.

✳ ✳ ✳

Across the street from the loading dock, at Portage College, sits the succinctly titled "College Seven." On several occasions as a preteen, I tried and failed to throw myself and my skateboard down these seven stair steps. The ground is rough. Always has been. Decades worth of snow and salt and rain will do that. Its dimpled, pebbled surface is primed for removing large chunks of your clothes and person.

I tell myself I could do it now. My body bigger, stronger, holding the experience of every stair set I've ollied down since the last time I stood at its peak—this body containing a life that's fared worse than a scraped knee. Past-me hadn't even worked a 9-5 yet. Never had to sit through a company-wide, all-hands meeting. Listen to a CEO burst into flames during the Q&A, contempt in their voice visceral as they scoffed at the notion of increased mental health benefits for their employees.

A "moral injury" is what my therapist calls that subsequent ache in the body. The desperate clenching of what might be a soul as it's crushed under the weight of living through late-stage capitalism and depression and who-knows-what other psychic ailments. Past-me broke his arm skateboarding once — a wound you can contain in plaster, how quaint.

But even that stifling angst can be cooled by pushing my skateboard down the street. It's a simple strategy I've used after arguments, breakups, layoffs, and deaths. The result isn't always total. Sometimes anger or despair seeps through the action, making my legs wobble, leaving what control I have over my board feeling untethered. But the weight is usually less, because it's hard for anything to stick to you if you're moving fast enough.

* * *

A few blocks away at the Provincial Building, where the Alberta Parks resides along with an array of Alberta Health Services programs, I pull up to a long sloping concrete ledge. Before I could ably ride a skateboard or understand the significance of the potential it proffered, my older half-brother took me here. He placed his skateboard at the top of the ledge, had me sit on it, then proceeded to guide me as I slid on it and down to the ledge's end. The goal? To scratch the graphic from his board, giving the illusion that he'd put it to serious use so he could later boast to his friends about all of the tricks he'd done.

I was a willing accomplice in this grift. Giddy, even. I tried to do the same with my board, but my brother told me no one would believe me because I wasn't good enough yet, so we left. Which, in retrospect, was true. If you're going to lie, you need to make sure the lie's not too much bigger than you are. That you can fit inside of it and still look casual.

In essence, that's how skateboarding works. Same with grieving. It's the only way you move forward: stretching your physical and mental limits inches at a time by playing fast and loose with the facts. Can you kickflip down those four stairs? Bring yourself to socialize after a terrible heartbreak? No. But can you kickflip off of a curb? Order an Americano from a barista? Pretty much. So, just exaggerate what you already know. A curb isn't much lower than four stairs if you think about it. Think harder. Talking to five people is essentially a watered-down conversation with one. Maybe think less. Push. Leap into a new place of being.

The four steps that lead up to the front entrance of St. Catherine's Parish are ones I've begrudgingly climbed to Sunday Mass and later tossed myself and skateboard down countless times before. This church is where much of my family has been baptized, confirmed, married. A house of god, the home of the first four set I ever kickflipped, an accomplishment that kept my spirit fed for weeks. It's where a limited-capacity funeral service was held for my grandfather last year. From my apartment in Vancouver, I watched my uncles give eulogies via Facebook Live.

Standing in front of the church now, sizing up its stairs, I imagine I might look like a wary sheep hesitating to return to its flock—or just a creep, lurking. The duality of the skateboarder. Always existing between states of reverence and wrongdoing.

Such a mess of memories I have of this place. Ones of family and beginnings and endings and skateboarding and screaming *godfuckingdammit* underneath the church's big white cross while struggling to land my trick down its stairs. The nondescript concrete slabs of this town gave definition to my childhood and context to my present. They're where I went when I needed escape, and they showed me what I'd need to look for when struggling in the future.

Yes, this system is imperfect. It took years (and the privilege of professional help) before I'd learn to articulate my grief in words. The emotions and abstractions that rode with me. Their temperatures rose and fell. Feelings became contained, familiar, necessary; and I could call on them to help orient my moods with near precision, to help bring back the memory of riding away from that kickflip at St. Catherine's; it still returns to me clearer than nearly any face.

Except for my grandfather's. I can see him in detail as I close my eyes. His large droopy ears, slicked-back hair; and I can hear his gruff grumbles of words that were at once commanding and comforting. At the cemetery, the sun is heavy and air sticky as we all stand around the columbarium. The priest officiating the interment ceremony arrives late and begins his speech by immediately forgetting my grandfather's name.

"Ed. It's Edward," my grandmother snaps. My siblings and cousins and uncles and I exchange smirks. The ashes are placed into the smooth black marble structure and glued shut. I let tears fall down my face, listen to them hit my shoe. We'd been waiting for this moment since December. The family comforts one another. The sun stays hot. A thought wriggles into my brain and I can't remove it. I know it's just trying to help, this ever-consuming way I've grown to see the world, so I entertain it: I bet Grandpa's columbarium would grind so good.

INSTANCES OF BIRDS IN PERIL

INSTANCE #1

THE SEAGULL WAS CHOKING. Moments before, it had stood on the craggy shoreline, confidently plucking a starfish from the water. Then, with the aplomb of a suburban father flipping hamburger patties on the backyard grill, it tossed the echinoderm into the air, caught it in its beak, and attempted to swallow it whole. Two out of five arms didn't make it down. Those outside appeared to be waving as the bird shook its head up and down in a panic. I watched from the dock as the bird threw itself back and around at odd angles, the three points of the starfish already inside jutting from its throat like a trio of gulping Adam's apples. My thumb and forefinger spread out over my iPhone screen as I zoomed in to take photos of the bird's struggle, documenting its violent heaving until finally, mercifully, the starfish began to slip out, one arm at a time before a final whip of the neck ejected the pointed creature like a loogie. Swiping through the photos made the ordeal look like an experimental dance piece, the seagull contorting itself into strange, almost beautiful shapes. Language expressed through feathered form. Perhaps a comment on the strangling constraints of capitalism, the suffocating omniscience of modern technologies, or a rebuke of the helplessness that defines our broken democratic system: the bird choked by greed like the rest of us.

I put my phone back into my coveralls and reversed the forklift that was carrying barrels of oil cling-wrapped together on a pallet destined for a tugboat bobbing at the far end of the dock. Then the seagull picked up the starfish once more. The warning beep from the forklift not phasing the gull, it flipped the starfish into the air, this time catching it perfectly in its gaping beak. The gull's throat opened disturbingly wide as the bird spun in small circles, coaxing all of the starfish's arms down its gullet. The pair looked like a poorly rolled sleeping bag stuffed haphazardly into its cover. Each starfish arm poked outwards from inside the bird—this time, five Adam's apples that gulped and gulped until they swallowed themselves.

Instance #2

With the tide out, the rock shelf exposed its full length before dropping off sharply into the ocean. Barefoot steps had to be taken quickly, the stone searing from the sun. We lay on towels, passed a joint between us, cooking ourselves. Tankers moved slow in the distance. Dogs and dog owners padded past, maneuvering around pools and crevasses in the rock that caught receding water, crabs, and anemones that, if touched, would hold onto your finger like slimy, burbling infant humans.

I turned over and looked at the bird. It was standing in the same spot it had been in the last time I'd flipped positions a half hour earlier. It still had something in its beak. At first glance, I thought it was picking at seaweed, but why hold onto it for this long? I propped myself up on an elbow and squinted. A distant beeping played at the back of my mind. The dock. The forklift. The choking seagull from years before. Three starfish arms sat in its open mouth like a fat, pronged tongue. Unlike the other bird, this one wasn't fighting. It just stood there, defeated, likely having exhausted all options of getting the sentient pentagram into its belly. Its experimental dance piece ineffective and lacking direction.

If it couldn't dislodge the starfish, the bird would surely die. I rose from the rock, put my shoes on and made slow, short steps toward it. If the bird let me, I'd pull the starfish out so it could live to shit indiscriminately another day. Heel to toe. Soft, considered footfalls. The seagull waddled slowly backwards, dull eyes on me.

"Dude, I just want to help." I tried to explain as it turned around and waddled faster, webbed feet smacking off the rock.

"C'mon, you know you're in a bad spot. I know I'm a big scary human. If we put that aside, we can get that thing out of you and then I'll leave you alone." The seagull cocked its head, one beady eye on my red, bleary eyes—a moment of consideration. I crouched down and extended my hands as if waiting for a communion wafer.

"I know how hard it is to ask for help. I've been in the same position—well, not the exact same, obviously. But there have been times when I've been scared to reach out to others when I needed a hand. It's easy to think keeping your problems to yourself works, that you can just ignore them or will yourself through, but all it does is isolate you. For real, man.

"That's why I started going to a therapist. I was becoming so emotionally, I don't know, alone. Unable to communicate what I needed. Like, I'd get into an argument with my girlfriend and instead of trying to empathize with why she was upset and look within myself and try to figure out why I was feeling a certain way and try to untangle that mess of emotion, I'd just internalize that anger and confusion I was carrying. Which eventually turns an opportunity for growth and reflection into this heavy fog of despair and resentment, you know?"

The bird extended its wings and hopped toward the water.

"Seriously, the only one who's going to be hurt by your unwillingness to be vulnerable is you!" I shouted at the seagull. It continued to hop away as I neared. The rock narrowed where it dipped into the ocean, the bird now at its tip.

"Let me help you." My words soft and deflated as the seagull flapped into the air. It flew towards the Malaspina Galleries rock formation, starfish gag weighing it down awkwardly. A wing tip clipped the water and it stumbled through the sky like a broken kite before managing to right itself. An allegory for student loan debt, maybe. Perched on top of the stone wave of the gallery, a natural marvel carved by the water lapping at its base, the bird looked nowhere and everywhere at once.

INSTANCE #3-280

It had to be an anomaly—witnessing two seagulls in two separate places, five years apart, choking on starfish. It was surreal the first time and depressing the next. There was no way this could be commonplace. Why would the birds do this? Perhaps it was a sign of illness, similar to the way dogs eat grass to induce vomiting and rid themselves of whatever poison they'd lapped up. Because a starfish couldn't possibly be appealing—it's a geometric barnacle.

The internet told me otherwise. A Google video search of "Seagull Chokes on Starfish" got two hundred and eighty-one results. In one, a group of seagulls fight over a purple starfish. A "lucky" bird wins the skirmish and forces the thing inside itself as all the other gulls gawk. The woman filming on her phone doing an incredulous play-by-play.

"I cannot believe—I just cannot believe this. It's—the whole thing? The whole thing! Dave, look, it got the whole damn thing down!"

Another video was just a thirty-second vignette of a lone bird walking down a concrete path, the lighting gray and heavy. The seagull looked as forlorn as a seagull can, while a long, single arm poked from its gullet. A Scottish narrator asked it the same questions I did—*Why? Can I help?*—and got the same answer.

Then, in what appeared to be Somewhere, Florida, a group of children chased a choking seabird. They squealed as the gull speed-waddled into the ocean, and watched quietly as it floated away toward an unknown fate.

One could imagine seagulls have struggled with this for eternity. A common misstep, an avoidable demise. But they keep doing it. Why haven't they communicated this danger to one another? Passed a warning down from egg to bird to egg again? Sure, sometimes it works out, and through the hurt, thrashing, and threat to mortality, what they want becomes theirs. But even if they get it down, it sits in the gut in agonizing digestion. Beady eyes bigger than belly, bigger than mouth, bigger than life. Foresight a pair of smudged reading glasses.

I wiped mine off on my shirt and pressed play on another video to remind myself.

THANK YOUS

Thank you to Matt Bowes, Thea Bowering, Meredith Thompson, Claire Kelly, and everyone at NeWest Press for believing in this odd little collection of essays and helping to bring it to life.

Thank you to Hiller Goodspeed, whose wonderful art you can find on the cover and throughout this book.

Thank you to the places that published versions of these essays and the editors who made them shine, including *PRISM*, *Invisiblog*, *Maisonneuve Magazine*, *VICE*, *The Outline*, and *Catapult*.

Thank you to all the kind, desperate, and perverted Craigslist anons who unwittingly participated in "Trolling in The Name of Art."

Thank you to everyone who shared their stories with me for this book.

Thank you to my family and friends for the love and support.

Thank you, dear reader, for reading.

NOTES

"Misadventure, Probably Drowning" relied heavily on the stories documented in *Uranium City—The Last Boom Town* (Driftwood Publishers, 1993), written by Bernard Garnet McIntyre.

"The Big Dog in the Sky is Dirty" features quotes from:

https://bc.ctvnews.ca/devil-statue-prompts-public-art-discussion-1.2016244

https://giseleamantea.ca/projects/public-art/

https://www.change.org/p/vancouver-parks-board-stop-false-creek-south-statue

June Callwood's last interview is referenced in "Pink Field":

https://www.youtube.com/watch?v=DuifotGZ4pc&ab_channel=Strombo

While the website *Pooptime* referenced in "Amazing Facts About Camels" no longer exists, you can find a snapshot of its spirit via the Wayback Machine:

https://web.archive.org/web/20180824022148/https://pooptime.com/

Some of the disgusting tidbits mentioned in "A Brief History of People Finding Weird Shit in Their Ears" you can find here if you want to learn more for whatever twisted reason:

https://www.cbsnews.com/chicago/news/2-investigators-57-maggots-removed-from-nursing-home-patients-ear/

https://www.huffpost.com/entry/wade-scholte-parker-color_n_886985

You can read the details of Gail from gail.com's WIPO case mentioned in "The Last Wholesome Corner of The Internet" here:

https://www.wipo.int/amc/en/domains/decisions/html/2006/d2006-0655.html

The Atlantic and *The New Statesman* pieces referenced in "My Personal Medium, Brian Eno" are "The New Age of Astrology" by Julie Beck and "Why millennials are looking for meaning in tarot cards" by Amelia Tate.

"Who Pissed On My Balcony?" features quotes and information from a September 28, 2018 episode of *CBC Radio*'s Quirks and Quarks, an April 12, 2012 edition of *The Washington Post*'s "Answer Man" column, and the YouTube video "Gray Squirrels Mark Territory With Pee."

Cole Nowicki is the author of *Right, Down + Circle* (ECW Press, 2023), was the lead writer and researcher for the documentary series *Post Radical*, and writes Simple Magic, a weekly newsletter about skateboarding, the internet, and other means of escape. His essays have appeared in *The Walrus, Catapult, VICE, Maisonneuve*, and elsewhere.